THE RULES OF GOLF

ILLUSTRATED AND EXPLAINED

An official
publication of the
United States
Golf Association

THE RULES OF GOLF

ILLUSTRATED AND EXPLAINED BY

TOM WATSON

WITH FRANK HANNIGAN

RANDOM HOUSE
NEW YORK

Copyright © 1980 Random House, Inc.

The material from *The Rules of Golf* has been previously
published by the United States Golf Association.
Copyright © 1976 by United States Golf Association.
All rights reserved under International and
Pan-American Copyright Conventions. Published in the
United States by Random House, Inc., New York, and
Simultaneously in Canada by Random House of Canada
Limited, Toronto.

Photograph credits: p 88, *Philadelphia Evening Bulletin;*
p. 137, Lester Nehamkin; p. 142, U.P.I. (left), Will
Hertzberg (right).

Library of Congress Cataloging in Publication Data

Watson, Tom, 1949–
  The rules of golf illustrated and explained.

  1. Golf—Rules. I. Hannigan, Frank. II. Title.
GV971.W37   796.352′02′022   79–4758
ISBN 0–394–50740–1
ISBN 0–394–73908–6 pbk.

Manufactured in the United States of America
9876543

CONTENTS

ACKNOWLEDGMENTS

The Rules of Golf: Illustrated and Explained came to pass with the advice and consent of a bevy of knowledgeable, talented counselors.

It originated in the fertile mind of C. A. (Tony) Wimpfheimer of Random House, who proposed to John Laupheimer, the Deputy Executive Director of the United States Golf Association, that there be such a book. These two made the necessary arrangements.

Members of the staff of *Golf Digest* magazine are responsible for the appearance of the book and its illustrations. Art Director John Newcomb, a consummate professional, was both the designer and the photographer, and it seems to me that his graphic effects, which contribute so much to the deserved success and popularity of *Golf Digest,* work wonderfully well in the context of this book. Associate Editor Jerry Tarde, a reclaimed golf professional who went on to greater things after conquering Northwestern's Medill School of Journalism, supervised the creation of the Elmer Wexler illustrations and, in general, made things happen. Editor Nick Seitz, one of the game's most underrated 13-handicap players, was generally cheerful.

The USGA was typically generous in its cooperation. Among those in the USGA family who read the manuscript and offered helpful suggestions was Will F. Nicholson, Jr., chairman of the Rules of Golf Committee during the time when the book came to be. The manuscript was pored over and vastly improved by P. J. Boatwright, Jr., USGA Executive Director, who holds a unique place in the realm of golf by virtue of his extraordinary expertise when it comes to understanding and applying the Rules of Golf. Tom Meeks, the USGA director of Rules and Competitions, was a sharp-eyed reader of the final version of the manuscript.

Tom Watson.

INTRODUCTION

This book is based on the premise that an understanding of the Rules vastly enhances the enjoyment of playing the game. Its goal is to rid golfers of the notion that the Rules of Golf must remain one of life's insoluble mysteries.

Knowledge of the Rules makes the game easier to play. Precise and correct application often saves a stroke or two. Example: When a ball is unplayable in a *lateral* water hazard, the Rules allow for a drop on either side of the hazard. A drop on the side opposite to where the ball entered (an option unfamiliar to many golfers) may make the next shot a much easier one. The subconscious benefits are even more important. The golfer who confronts a delicate pitch shot over a bunker after dropping away from a cart path, uncertain as to whether or not he's dropped correctly, is robbed of the game's necessities—concentration and confidence.

The Rules of Golf are the joint responsibility of two organizations —the United States Golf Association and the Royal and Ancient Golf Club of St. Andrews, Scotland. They jointly write and interpret the Rules, and every national golf organization, professional and amateur, defers to their judgment. A formal agreement exists to the effect that neither the USGA nor the R&A will act unilaterally and that amendments will be adopted only every fourth year. This book is published as the 1980 changes take effect.

Formal interpretations, called *Decisions,* are issued by the USGA Rules of Golf Committee as a response to questions which defy resolution in the Rules proper. These questions, all dealing with actual situations, come from John Q. Weekend Golfer, both over the phone and in writing, from golf committees and associations, and quite a few derive from incidents on the professional tours which, in a sense, are the ultimate testing grounds for the Rules. The USGA will not answer hypothetical questions. These Decisions are published and codified at the rate of about thirty a year and are considered as binding precedents; (69-20) in parentheses refers to the 20th Decision issued in 1969.

Other key elements of the style of the book are abbreviations, so that "R 17-1" means that whatever I'm writing about in that instance stems from the first clause of Rule 17. Similarly, "Def. 30" means it's coming at you courtesy of Definition 30.

The primary tools in this book are the 41 Rules, which are printed in their entirety. Supplementary text after each Rule falls into four general categories:

Rationales—why the dreaded stroke-and-distance penalty for a lost ball makes sense, difficult as that may be to swallow when you return to the tee after the ball you drove is lost and the next stroke is your third rather than your second.

*Mild exhortations—*i.e., *do* become familiar with the Definitions.

*Clarifications—*i.e., summaries of USGA Decisions that have been selected expressly in the hope that they will sprout and flourish in the memory of those of us who find it easier to learn by example than by rote.

*Live examples—*i.e., how it came about that Johnny Miller was penalized two strokes for carrying an 18-inch-long putter that he never used.

Since this is *The Rules of Golf: Illustrated and Explained,* photographs and diagrams are sprinkled throughout the book whenever a graphic illustration might alleviate the learning process.

I have not aimed the book at any one segment of golfers. While it assumes at least a basic and primary understanding of golf terminology, beginners, too, can profit immeasurably from this experience, although they're going to have to work a little harder at it. Occasionally they'll encounter a word or phrase that is explained further on. For example, there are references to both "match play" and "stroke play" in the text after Rule 4, but the explanations of "match play" and "stroke play" await their natural occurrence in Rules 6 and 7.

The viewpoint of this book is unashamedly traditional and conservative. There is only one set of Rules and here they are. "Winter Rules," which permit the golfer to improve the lie by moving the ball, are an abomination and should be shunned except when it is otherwise not possible to play at all. Those who lament that the Rules, strictly observed, are sometimes unfair and onerous miss the crucial point that the true satisfaction of golf comes from accepting, meeting and overcoming a challenge. The smaller the challenge met, the smaller the satisfaction gained.

The very nature of an activity meandering over a hundred and fifty irregular acres as contrasted with one confined to a flat and precisely defined rectangle (as in tennis, basketball or football) does suggest a need for a complicated set of procedures. When Earl Campbell of the Houston Oilers is driven out of bounds by a horde of tacklers on the four-yard line of the Dallas Cowboys, we all know instinctively that the Oilers' next play will begin on the Cowboy four. But suppose a golf ball falls into a stream just short of a green and is carried out of bounds by the rush of water. Is that ball out of bounds or is it to be regarded as a ball lost in a water hazard—or both? (Readers without patience can skip to the text that accompanies Rule 33.)

However, too much shouldn't be made of such strange if intriguing incidents. The Rules-shy golfer will go a long way toward understanding them by grasping three principles enunciated years ago by

Richard S. Tufts, a former USGA President. Mr. Tufts said the principles underlying the Rules are:

1. Play the ball as it lies.
2. Play the course as you find it.
3. When it's not possible to do either, do what's fair.

Of course, the question of what is fair leads to some lively debates. Given the intensity of feelings about the sport (British Prime Minister Arthur Balfour's definition of the game was "the true and adequate end of man's existence"), it is remarkable that the playing rules are the same in all sixty golf-playing countries. Moreover, the same code works for and is accepted by those of us on the professional tours as well as 40-handicap amateurs.

This isn't to say that the Rules are perfect. On the contrary, every golfer who thinks about them at all—including the Rules-makers themselves—has a pet peeve. At the same time, all thinking golfers agree that it's a better game if we all use the *same* Rules.

1

ETIQUETTE

COURTESY ON THE COURSE

Consideration for Other Players

In the interest of all, players should play without delay.

No player should play until the players in front are out of range.

Players searching for a ball should signal the players behind them to pass as soon as it becomes apparent that the ball will not easily be found: they should not search for five minutes before doing so. They should not continue play until the players following them have passed and are out of range.

When the play of a hole has been completed, players should immediately leave the putting green.

Behavior During Play

No one should move, talk or stand close to or directly behind the ball or the hole when a player is addressing the ball or making a stroke.

The player who has the honor should be allowed to play before his opponent or fellow-competitor tees his ball.

PRIORITY ON THE COURSE

In the absence of special rules, two-ball matches should have precedence of and be entitled to pass any three- or four-ball match.

A single player has no standing and should give way to a match of any kind.

Any match playing a whole round is entitled to pass a match playing a shorter round.

If a match fails to keep its place on the course and loses more than one clear hole on the players in front, it should allow the match following to pass.

CARE OF THE COURSE

Holes in Bunkers

Before leaving a bunker, a player should carefully fill up and smooth over all holes and footprints made by him.

Restore Divots, Repair Ball-Marks and Damage by Spikes

Through the green, a player should ensure that any turf cut or displaced by him is replaced at once and pressed down, and that any damage to the putting green made by the ball is carefully repaired. Damage to the putting green caused by golf shoe spikes should be repaired *on completion of the hole*.

Damage to Greens—Flagsticks, Bags, etc.

Players should insure that, when putting down bags, or

(continued)

the flagstick, no damage is done to the putting green, and that neither they nor their caddies damage the hole by standing close to it, in handling the flagstick or in removing the ball from the hole. The flagstick should be properly replaced in the hole before the players leave the putting green. Players should not damage the putting green by leaning on their putters, particularly when removing the ball from the hole.

Golf Carts

Local Notices regulating the movement of golf carts should be strictly observed.

Damage Through Practice Swings

In taking practice swings, players should avoid causing damage to the course, particularly the tees, by removing divots.

Etiquette involves the rules of conduct which ought to guide golfers in their relations with one another. Ours is a sensitive, perhaps even a fragile, game. If it is to prosper or be fun to play (which may be the highest form of prosperity), golfers have to be decent to one another and to the course.

The relationship between the golfer and the course is fascinating. I can't think of another sport in which the playing arena must be maintained, in part, by the players. In golf we take it for granted that the player has the responsibility for performing the elementary housekeeping chores of replacing divots, repairing ball marks and smoothing bunkers.

There is, however, a provision of the Etiquette section which is often ignored, or so it seems to me. That's the very first one, which reads: "In the interest of all, players should play without delay."

Slow play is golf's disease. Four players in the same group should never need more than four hours to play 18 holes of golf. The five-hour round is a desecration, and it says much for the appeal of the game that, hating the prospect though they must, golfers go right on playing.

I don't think there's any correlation between scores and pace of play. It's not necessary to agonize over shots in order to shoot sub-par scores. At the same time, the high-handicap player has no excuse for dawdling. I have friends who can't break 100, but we can play together without feeling that we're holding one another up.

I have a reputation for being one of the fastest players on the pro tour. I began to play golf with my father when I was eight years old and with the clear-cut understanding that I was more than welcome, provided I kept up. So I became a fast player at a very early age.

2

DEFINITIONS

THE DEFINITIONS

The single most helpful piece of advice available to those who want to understand the Rules of Golf better is this: *Read the Definitions.*

The Definitions are basic. They exist because many key words and special terms in the Rules are not those we use in everyday language and must therefore be clarified.

Golfers tend to resort to the Rules only when they have a problem and are in a hurry for an answer. They'll run into a phrase such as "through the green" and the mind tends to boggle. It doesn't help, of course, that "through the green" is often misused by television commentators to apply to balls hit *beyond* the green, when it means something entirely different (see Def. 35).

So become familiar with the Definitions. You don't have to memorize them, but find out where they are and be prepared to refer back to them. You should accept the help given by the Rules themselves when they steer you back to the Definitions. Suppose, for example, there's an incident involving the movement of a ball after it's come to rest. The Index (under "Ball—Moved or Moving") will direct you to Rule 27, which deals with six general instances, two others that apply in match play, and another for stroke play. But the *first* thing to determine is: Did the ball in fact move? What does "move" mean? If the ball jiggles but doesn't actually go anywhere, has it been moved? See Definition 3, just as the heading for Rule 27—"Ball at Rest Moved (Def. 3)"—suggests.

The Definitions follow, punctuated by occasional comments which are inserted for the purpose of, if you'll pardon the expression, defining the Definitions.

DEFINITION 1: ADDRESSING THE BALL	A player has "addressed the ball" when he has taken his stance (Definition 29) and has also grounded his club, except that in a hazard a player has addressed the ball when he has taken his stance.

DEFINITION 2: ADVICE	"Advice" is any counsel or suggestion which could influence a player in determining his play, the choice of a club, or the method of making a stroke. Information on the Rules or Local Rules is not advice.

Advice includes giving another player an instructional tip during a round.

DEFINITION 3: BALL DEEMED TO MOVE	A ball is deemed to have "moved" if it leave its position and come to rest in any other place.

A ball has *not* moved if it only jiggles or oscillates.

When It's Wise Not to Address a Ball

If a ball teeters on a slope anywhere outside a hazard, it makes sense to play the next stroke without addressing the ball, since if the ball moves after address, the player is deemed to have caused it to move and incurs a penalty stroke. Note that I have not addressed the ball because the club has not been grounded. If it moves, and I haven't caused it to move, there's no penalty and I would play the ball from where it then lies. This advice doesn't apply within a hazard, where address is completed as soon as the stance is taken. (Def. 1 and R. 27-1f)

DEFINITION 4:

BALL HOLED

A ball is "holed" when it lies within the circumference of the hole and all of it is below the level of the lip of the hole.

DEFINITION 5:

BALL IN PLAY, PROVISIONAL BALL, WRONG BALL

a. A ball is "in play" as soon as the player has made a stroke on the teeing ground. It remains as his ball in play until holed out, except when it is out of bounds, lost or lifted, or another ball has been substituted under an applicable Rule or Local Rule: a ball so substituted becomes the ball in play.

b. A "provisional ball" is a ball played under Rule 30 for a ball which may be lost outside a water hazard or may be out of bounds. It ceases to be a provisional ball when the Rule
(continued)

19

provides *either* that the player continue play with it as the ball in play *or* that it be abandoned.

c. A "wrong ball" is any ball other than the ball in play or a provisional ball or, in stroke play, a second ball played under Rule 11-5 or under Rule 21-3d.

There can only be one ball "in play" for one player at one time. If a player's ball heads in the direction of a water hazard and the player drops and plays another ball, the second ball is then "in play." If the player finds the original to be playable and plays it, he has played a "wrong ball."

The phrase "provisional ball" is often confused with "second ball" in Rule 11-5. The former is a ball you may play in order to save time when your ball *may* be lost (not in a water hazard) or out of bounds but you're not sure; the latter is a ball you are allowed to play in stroke play when you are doubtful of your rights or the proper procedure.

Key point: You may *not* play a provisional ball for the reason that the ball may be lost in a water hazard.

DEFINITION 6:
BALL LOST

A ball is "lost" if:

a. It be not found, or be not identified as his by the player, within five minutes after the player's side or his or their caddies have begun to search for it; *or*

b. The player has put another ball into play under the Rules, even though he may not have searched for the original ball;

c. The player has played any stroke with a provisional ball from a point nearer the hole than the place where the original ball is likely to be, whereupon the provisional ball becomes the ball in play.

Time spent in playing a wrong ball is not counted in the five minute period allowed for search.

Here's what some key Decisions on the subject of lost balls say:

● A player searches for his ball for two minutes, declares his ball is lost and heads back toward the tee. Before he drops another ball and within the five-minute search period, his caddie finds his first ball.

As the player had *not* put another ball in play under the Rules, he could play the first ball. (62-28)

● Harold Oatman, a Norfolk, Virginia, pro, asked what happens in stroke play when a player searches for a ball for less than five minutes, gives up the search, returns to the tee and plays another ball. The original ball is then found. The player picks up the second ball and plays the first.

The original was lost when the player put a second ball in play—no matter how long the search. When he lifted the second ball he violated Rule 27-1c (one-stroke penalty). When he played a stroke with the original ball he played a wrong ball (two more strokes under

Rule 21-3a.) Finally, if he doesn't rectify the mistake by replacing the second ball before he plays from the next tee, he's disqualified under Rule 21-3b. (56-18)

● Jimmy Thomson, reputedly the longest hitter in the world during the 1930s, asked how to rule when two players are playing identical balls, i.e., balls of the same brand and marking and with the same numbers. The balls come to rest very close together, and the players are not sure of the ownership of either.

It may seem harsh, but both balls are to be treated as lost, since neither player can identify one as his. A pencil mark or a dot made by a marking pen in a dimple is all it takes to identify a ball properly. (56-25)

● Ralph Meyer, of San Marcos, California, wrote that on his course, on a par-3 hole, a player hit wildly, and thinking his original might be lost, played a provisional ball. The result with the provisional ball was excellent. In fact, it came to rest one inch from the hole. Must the player search for the original ball?

No. He can tap the ball near the hole in for a 4. (67-13)

An incident on the tour involving Miller Barber led to these two:

● A player is reasonably certain that his ball is high up in a tree but he can't see it and therefore can't identify it. The ball is lost. (75-7)

● A player can see *a* ball in a tree but can't retrieve it to identify it as his.

The ball is lost (which means the player is not allowed to treat it as unplayable; he must suffer the stroke-and-distance penalty). (75-7)

DEFINITION 7:

CADDIE, FORECADDIE AND EQUIPMENT

a. A "caddie" is one who carries or handles a player's clubs during play and otherwise assists him in accordance with the Rules.

When one caddie is employed by more than one player, he is always deemed to be the caddie of the player whose ball is involved, and equipment carried by him is deemed to be that player's equipment, except when the caddie acts upon specific directions of another player, in which case he is considered to be that other player's caddie.

Note: *In threesome, foursome, best-ball and four-ball play, a caddie carrying for more than one player should be assigned to the members of one side.*

b. A "forecaddie" is one employed by the Committee to indicate to players the position of balls on the course, and is an outside agency (Definition 22).

c. "Equipment" is anything used, worn or carried by or for the player except his ball in play. Equipment includes a golf cart. If such a cart is shared by more than one player, its status under the Rules is the same as that of a caddie employed by more than one player.

Golf carts subject the Rules to strains. There is a USGA Decision, 70-17, which takes up six full pages in the "Decisions on the Rules of Golf" tomes. A few, but by no means all, of the elements in 70-17 are:

*In a single match A and B, opponents, share a cart. The cart is parked when A shanks a ball and it strikes the cart. A loses the hole. It doesn't matter who drove the cart up to the point where it was parked.

*A is driving and runs over his own ball. Since A was directing the cart, he incurs a penalty of one stroke and must replace his ball. See Rule 27-1d.

*A is driving and runs over B's ball. A's incurs a penalty of one stroke under Rule 27-2a and B must replace his ball *unless* the incident occurred during a search for B's ball. In that case, there's no penalty. See Rule 27-1b.

Now it's a four-ball match and A and B are partners and share a cart. (A four-ball match is two against two. Definition 28 up ahead tells us so.)

*A drives over his own ball. A incurs a penalty of one stroke and the ball shall be replaced. B, his partner, is not penalized.

*A drives over B's ball. B incurs a penalty of one stroke (Rule 40-3e), but A is not penalized.

*A drives over an opponent's ball. Rule 40-3f governs, so that A is penalized one stroke but B is not penalized.

*A's ball hits the cart A and B are sharing. A is disqualified for the hole; B incurs no penalty (Rule 40-3b).

*C's ball hits the cart A and B are sharing. There is no penalty under the revised 1980 Rules. C can either play his ball as it lies or replay the stroke.

DEFINITION 8: CASUAL WATER	"Casual water" is any temporary accumulation of water which is visible before or after the player takes his stance and is not in a water hazard. Snow and ice are either casual water or loose impediments, at the option of the player.

Note that soft mushy ground, or mud, does not of itself constitute casual water.

DEFINITION 9: COMMITTEE	The "Committee" is the committee in charge of the competition or, if the matter does not arise in a competition, the committee in charge of the course.

In everyday informal play the Committee is not likely to be available. The golf professional is usually authorized to act on behalf of the Committee.

DEFINITION 10: COMPETITOR	A "competitor" is a player in a stroke competition. A "fellow-competitor" is any person with whom the competitor plays. Neither is partner of the other. In stroke play foursome and four-ball competitions, where the context so admits, the word "competitor" or "fellow-competitor" shall be held to include his partner.

"Competitor" is a nice old-fashioned and useful word which we seem to avoid. The people with whom you are playing in stroke play are "fellow-competitors." Calling them "playing partners" is inaccurate and can lead to misunderstandings, since the word "partner" suggests someone with whom you are in business and can assist.

DEFINITION 11:

COURSE

The "course" is the whole area within which play is permitted. It is the duty of the Committee to define its boundaries accurately.

What happens when a Committee is lax and fails to define "out of bounds" accurately? Confusion is what happens, not to mention arguments. That's why it's important for someone always to be available who can speak for the Committee, and that someone is customarily the club professional.

DEFINITION 12:

FLAGSTICK

The "flagstick" is a movable straight indicator provided by the Committee, with or without bunting or other material attached, centered in the hole to show its position. It shall be circular in cross-section.

DEFINITION 13:

GROUND UNDER REPAIR

"Ground under repair" is any portion of the course so marked by order of the Committee or so declared by its authorized representative. It includes material piled for removal and a hole made by a greenkeeper, even if not so marked. Stakes and lines defining ground under repair are in such ground.

Note: *Grass cuttings and other material left on the course*
(continued)

When Is a Ball in Ground Under Repair?
The ball is in an area marked ground under repair because it touches the line. I'd be entitled to take relief even if my ball was outside the area, but my stance put one of my feet on the line. This is one of the changes made in the 1980 Rules. (Def. 13)

> *which have been abandoned and are not intended to be removed are not ground under repair unless so marked.*

Ground under repair is customarily and best defined by white lines. When a ball touches the white line it is considered in ground under repair and the relief offered in Rule 32 can be obtained. Prior to 1980 this was not the case.

A couple of interpretations of Definition 13:

● Delbert Talley, Green Committee Chairman at The Country Club of Terre Haute, Indiana, wanted to know if a rut or a groove made by a maintenance vehicle is considered a hole made by a greenkeeper.

No, but a player whose ball is in a deep rut would be justified in asking the Committee to declare the rut to be ground under repair, and the Committee would be justified in doing so. (55-48)

● What's the status of a tree stump?, wondered Mrs. Robert J. Williamson, of Baton Rouge, Louisiana.

There is no free relief from a tree stump not marked as ground under repair unless it is in the process of being unearthed or cut up, in which case it is "material piled for removal" and thus ground under repair. (69-20)

DEFINITION 14:

HAZARDS

A "hazard" is any bunker, water hazard or lateral water hazard. Bare patches, scrapes, roads, tracks and paths are not hazards.

It is the duty of the Committee to define accurately the extent of the water hazards. That part of a water hazard to be played as a lateral water hazard should be distinctively marked. Stakes and lines defining the margins of hazards are in the hazards.

a. A "bunker" is an area of bare ground, often a depression, which is usually covered with sand. Grass-covered ground bordering or within a bunker is *not* part of the hazard.

b. A "water hazard" is any sea, lake, pond, river, ditch, surface drainage ditch or other open water course (regardless of whether or not it contains water), and anything of a similar nature. All ground or water within the margin of a water hazard, whether or not it be covered with any growing substance, is part of the water hazard. The margin of a water hazard is deemed to extend vertically upwards.

c. A "lateral water hazard" is a water hazard or that part of a water hazard so situated that it is not possible or is deemed by the Committee to be impracticable to drop a ball behind the water hazard and keep the spot at which the ball last crossed the margin of the hazard between the player and the hole.

Note: *Water hazards should be defined by yellow stakes or lines and lateral water hazards by red stakes or lines.*

Grass in a Bunker
The Rules allow you to ground your club in a bunker in a grassy area within the bunker. Grass-covered ground within a bunker is not considered part of the hazard. (Def. 14a)

Watch your language! Those areas of bare ground covered with sand are "bunkers"—not "sand traps." And learn to think in terms of "lateral water hazard" rather than the misnomer "parallel water hazard."

Stakes used to define hazards are obstructions and may be removed when they interfere, but as Definition 20 will reveal, stakes defining boundaries may *not* be moved.

There is some understandable confusion about the proper names for and distinctions between types of water hazards. Think of it this way: there are only two kinds. The most common is, quite simply, a "water hazard," and it is often called a "regular water hazard." The other is a "lateral water hazard." The problem with understanding this definition is that a "lateral water hazard" does not necessarily have to run lateral, or parallel, to the line of play. It's up to the Committee to make the distinction and the Committee should be guided by the principle of whether or not it's fair or practicable to drop behind the hazard and keep the spot at which the ball last crossed the margin between the player and the hole. If not, the hazard should be categorized as "lateral" so that the player can avail himself of the extra options expressed in Rule 33-3.

DEFINITION 15:

HOLE

> The "hole" shall be 4¼ inches in diameter and at least 4 inches deep. If a lining be used, it shall be sunk at least 1 inch below the putting green surface unless the nature of the soil makes it impractical to do so; its outer diameter shall not exceed 4¼ inches.

DEFINITION 16:

HONOR

> The side which is entitled to play first from the teeing ground is said to have the "honor."

DEFINITION 17:

LOOSE IMPEDIMENTS

> The term "loose impediments" denotes natural objects not fixed or growing and not adhering to the ball, and includes stones not solidly embedded, leaves, twigs, branches and the like, dung, worms and insects and casts or heaps made by them.
>
> Snow and ice are either casual water or loose impediments, at the option of the player.
>
> Sand and loose soil are loose impediments on the putting green, but not elsewhere on the course.

How "solidly embedded" does a stone have to be in order not to qualify as a loose impediment? The USGA says that partially embedded stones that may be picked up *with ease* qualify as loose impediments.

A common violation occurs when a player's ball is on the apron, he wants to putt, and there's some sand on the apron on his line to the hole. The sand is brushed aside. Violation! To qualify as loose impediments, sand must be *on* the putting green.

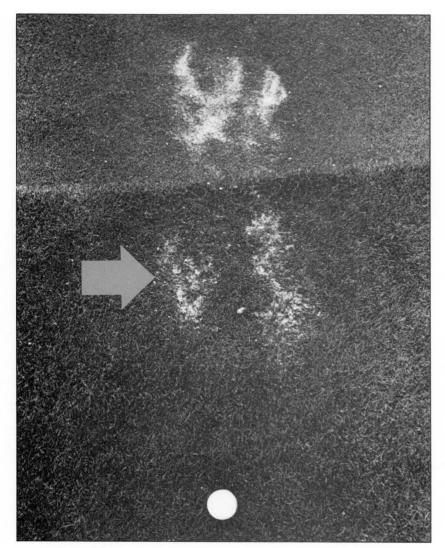

When Sand Can't Be Removed
Sand has been splashed from a bunker both onto a putting green (arrow) and on the apron just off the green. Both areas are on my line to the hole and might affect the roll. Nevertheless, the sand off the green is not a loose impediment and may not be moved; the sand on the green is a loose impediment and may be removed. (Def. 17, R. 17-1, and R. 18)

A query by Mrs. Robert I. Lacey, of Great Neck, New York, led to one of the classic USGA Decisions. She asked if a half-eaten pear in front of a ball in a hazard is considered a natural object or an artificial object. If it's natural and therefore a loose impediment, it can't be moved; if it's artificial (and thus an "obstruction" under Definition 20), it can be removed without penalty under Rule 31. The hazard in which the pear was lodged is not in close proximity of the pear tree.

A: If the player removed the pear, she violated Rule 33-1, the penalty for which is: Match play—Loss of hole; Stroke play—Two strokes.

A pear is a natural object (an obstruction must be artificial). When detached from a tree it is a loose impediment under Definition 17 and may not be removed from a hazard. The fact that someone had partially eaten the pear in question and that it was foreign to its natural

27

area does not alter the case.

Natural objects may be transformed into obstructions (Definition 20) through processes of manufacturing or construction. For example: a log (loose impediment) which has been split and has had legs attached to it has been changed by construction into a bench (obstruction); or a piece of coal (loose impediment) is considered an obstruction after it has been manufactured into a charcoal briquet. However, a loose impediment does not become an obstruction merely because it may have been slightly *altered by man. If it were otherwise, a player might declare that a twig broken by a man's footstep is an obstruction. (59-40)*

DEFINITION 18:
MARKER

A "marker" is a scorer in stroke play who is appointed by the Committee to record a competitor's score. He may be a fellow-competitor. He is not a referee.

A marker should not lift a ball or mark its position unless authorized to do so by the competitor and, unless he is a fellow-competitor, should not attend the flagstick or stand at the hole or mark its position.

The marker in stroke play today is invariably a fellow-competitor. On the PGA tour you may have noticed someone, usually in a uniform, walking with each group of players and recording scores. Her function is to report the scores at the end of each hole to a telephone operator. The scores she reports are the source material for television and the scoreboards, but they are *not* official.

There's no such thing as a marker in match play. Keeping a hole-by-hole card in match play is a useful way of tracking the match, but the card has no official status.

DEFINITION 19:
OBSERVER

An "observer" is appointed by the Committee to assist a referee to decide questions of fact and to report to him any breach of a Rule or Local Rule. An observer should not attend the flagstick, stand at or mark the position of the hole, or lift the ball or mark its position.

DEFINITION 20:
OBSTRUCTIONS

An "obstruction" is anything artificial, whether erected, placed or left on the course, including the artificial surfaces and sides of roads and paths but excepting:—

a. Objects defining out of bounds, such as walls, fences, stakes and railings;

b. In water hazards, artificially surfaced banks or beds, including bridge supports when part of such a bank. Bridges and bridge supports which are not part of such a bank are obstructions;

c. Any construction declared by the Committee to be an integral part of the course.

No Relief from Boundary Fence or Stakes

Even though it's artificial, an out-of-bounds fence is not an obstruction. Moreover, boundary fences and stakes are regarded as "things fixed" and may not be moved. When a ball is up against an out-of-bounds fence or stake and can't be played, there's nothing to do except declare the ball unplayable and accept a penalty stroke. (Def. 20, R. 17-1 and R. 29-2)

Definition 20b often stops readers cold, with the phrase "artificially surfaced banks or beds." Assume you're in a water hazard and your ball is playable but a stone-and-concrete wall inside the hazard interferes with your swing. That stone-and-concrete wall, put there to prevent erosion, is an artificially surfaced bank; it is *not* an obstruction and you don't get relief from it without penalty.

Definition 20c gives the Committee latitude to preserve the character of a hole which might be lost if free relief was given from something artificial on that hole. The best-known case occurs on the 17th hole—the Road Hole—of the Old Course at St. Andrews in Scotland. When you miss the green to the right, the ball invariably winds up on the blacktop road adjacent to and well below the green. When I'm on the road, I pray to get down in three. The road makes the 17th hole at St. Andrews one of the great par-4 holes anywhere. It would be spoiled if a ball could be dropped from the road without penalty.

DEFINITION 21:
OUT OF BOUNDS

"Out of bounds" is ground on which play is prohibited.

When out of bounds is fixed by stakes or a fence, the out of bounds line is determined by the nearest inside points of the stakes or fence posts at ground level; the line is deemed to extend vertically upwards. When out of bounds is fixed by a line on the ground, the line itself is out of bounds.

A ball is out of bounds when all of it lies out of bounds.

The logic of the Rules of Golf is usually inescapable. Take the boundary definition of a line running between the inside (golf-course side) points of stakes or fence posts. Why not the outside points to give us a break? Because it might require climbing a fence, and it might involve trespassing, that's why.

DEFINITION 22:
OUTSIDE AGENCY

An "outside agency" is any agency not part of the match or, in stroke play, not part of a competitor's side, and includes a referee, a marker, an observer, or a forecaddie employed by the Committee. Neither wind nor water is an outside agency.

Golf balls are deflected by and moved by alien objects and beings, such as dogs, spectators and trash containers. Those are called "outside agencies," and within the body of the Rules you'll find what to do, depending on the circumstance, when an outside agency intrudes.

DEFINITION 23:
PARTNER

A "partner" is a player associated with another player on the same side.

In a threesome, foursome or a four-ball where the context so admits, the word "player" shall be held to include his partner.

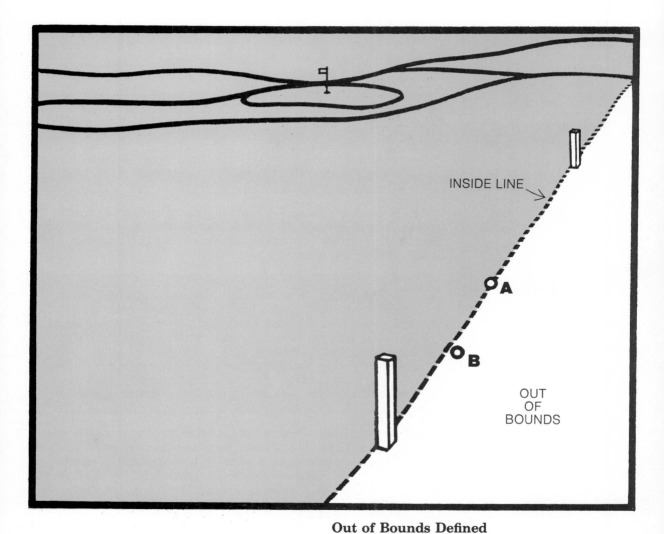

INSIDE LINE

OUT
OF
BOUNDS

Out of Bounds Defined
*When stakes are used to
define out of bounds, the
boundary line is determined
by the nearest inside edges
of the stakes (see dotted
line). Since a ball is not out
of bounds unless all of it is
out of bounds, Ball A is in
bounds; Ball B is out of
bounds. (Def. 21)*

DEFINITION 24:

PENALTY STROKE

A "penalty stroke" is one added to the score of a side under certain Rules. It does not affect the order of play.

DEFINITION 25:

PUTTING GREEN

The "putting green" is all ground of the hole being played which is specially prepared for putting or otherwise defined as such by the Committee.

A ball is deemed to be on the putting green when any part of it touches the putting green.

An "apron" or "collar," a narrow strip cut nearly as low as the greens, is not considered part of the putting green. The words "apron" and "collar" are examples of everyday golf language which is not used in the Rules.

DEFINITION 26:

REFEREE

A "referee" is a person who has been appointed by the Committee to accompany players to decide questions of fact and of golf law. He shall act on any breach of Rule or Local Rule which he may observe or which may be reported to him by an observer (Definition 19).

In stroke play the Committee may limit a referee's duties.

A referee should not attend the flagstick, stand at or mark the position of the hole, or lift the ball or mark its position.

Very few golfers ever have the opportunity to play with a referee accompanying them. It's too bad, because the presence of a referee seems to put the game on a slightly higher plane. Referees can enhance the final matches of club championships, provided they're competent. The USGA offers a fascinating booklet for the bargain price of 25¢ on the subject called "Duties of Officials Under the Rules of Golf." (Write to USGA, Far Hills, N.J. 07931.)

DEFINITION 27:

RUB OF THE GREEN

A "rub of the green" occurs when a ball in motion is accidentally stopped or deflected by any outside agency.

DEFINITION 28:

SIDES AND MATCHES

SIDE: A player, or two or more players who are partners.
SINGLE: A match in which one plays against another.
THREESOME: A match in which one plays against two, and each side plays one ball.
FOURSOME: A match in which two play against two, and each side plays one ball.
THREE-BALL: A match in which three play against one another, each playing his own ball.
BEST-BALL: A match in which one plays against the better ball of two or the best ball of three players.

(continued)

> FOUR-BALL: A match in which two play their better ball against the better ball of two other players.
> **Note:** *In a best-ball or four-ball match, if a partner be absent for reasons satisfactory to the Committee, the remaining member(s) of his side may represent the side.*

I'm something of a traditionalist and am therefore among the minority in the United States who believe we should cling to the proper usage of the terms in Definition 28 and fight the good, if losing, fight against the bastardization of these terms. Thus:

*A threesome is *not* three who are playing together; it's a form of competition virtually extinct.

*A foursome is a fascinating kind of competition in which partners play alternate strokes. It is *not* four players who are playing together. This form of play is sometimes and unnecessarily referred to as a "Scotch Foursome."

*A four-ball is by far the most popular form of golf played in this country. Alas, too often it's called a "best-ball," which, again, is an interesting but out-of-vogue kind of match covered in Rule 40.

DEFINITION 29:

STANCE

> Taking the "stance" consists in a player placing his feet in position for and preparatory to making a stroke.

DEFINITION 30:

STIPULATED ROUND

> The "stipulated round" consists of playing the holes of the course in their correct sequence unless otherwise authorized by the Committee. The number of holes in a stipulated round is 18 unless a smaller number is authorized by the Committee.
>
> In match play only, the Committee may, for the purpose of settling a tie, extend the stipulated round to as many holes as are required for a match to be won.

This gives us an excuse to reprint the USGA's famous Stipulated Round Decision. The opponents were vying in a tournament run by the Women's Central Pennsylvania Golf Association:

Q: In match play, two women were so busy talking they failed to play two holes. They did not realize the omission until the results of the match were posted and they wondered why their scores were so good. It was too late in the day to send them out again to play the whole 18, and to wait until the following day to replay their match would have delayed the whole flight and upset the entire tournament schedule. We sent them out immediately after their error was discovered to play the two holes they had left out, and we are anxious to know whether or not this was correct. Unfortunately, those two holes changed the result of the match, and there has been considerable discussion as to whether our ruling was legal.

What is the correct ruling in such a case? Also, what would be the correct ruling in stroke play?

A: The Committee's decision is final—see Rule 11-3.

However, the Committee should not have directed that the two omitted holes be played belatedly, especially if this were to have been done out of correct sequence—see Definition 30.

The result should have been allowed to stand as originally posted —see Rule 11-1. Had the players agreed to play less than the stipulated round, both would have been subject to disqualification—see Rule 4.

In stroke play, both players would be disqualified for failing to play the stipulated round—see Rules 1 and 7-1 and Definition 30. (61-7)

DEFINITION 31:
STROKE

A "stroke" is the forward movement of the club made with the intention of fairly striking at and moving the ball.

What a succinct and valuable piece of information comes to us in Definition 31. The key words are "forward" and "intention." A smattering of Decisions having to do with strokes:

● Norman Beecher, of Clearwater, Florida, put a question this way: A player begins the forward movement of the club with the intention of hitting the ball but stops his swing before he has progressed halfway.

The answer: Since the player's intention to move the ball died before he was able to move it, there was no stroke. (55-10)

● Norman Falkner, captain of the Weston Golf and Country Club, Toronto, Canada, asked for confirmation of a club ruling he'd made (correctly): In a mixed foursome competition, it was the woman's turn to play a stroke requiring a long carry over water. Her partner counseled her to "whiff" the ball, promising to put the ball on the green with his next stroke. The woman's "whiff" was not a stroke, since she did not intend to strike the ball. Her partner therefore played out of turn. (55-54)

● Is it permissible to play a left-handed stroke with the back of a right-handed club? asked C. R. Ault, of Birmingham, Alabama.
Yes. (59-19)

DEFINITION 32:
TEEING

In "teeing," the ball may be placed on the ground, on an irregularity of surface created by the player on the ground or on sand or other substance in order to raise it off the ground.

DEFINITION 33:
TEEING GROUND

The "teeing ground" is the starting place for the hole to be played. It is a rectangular area two club-lengths in depth, the front and the sides of which are defined by the outside limits of two tee-markers. A ball is outside the teeing ground when all of it lies outside the stipulated area.

When playing the first stroke with any ball (including a
(continued)

Stroke or No Stroke?

Many golfers believe that as soon as the club starts away from the ball the stroke has begun. Not so! There's no stroke until the club moves forward with intent. I've started my stroke in the right-hand picture. Even so, if something disturbs me and I can check my swing before the club head reaches the ball, it doesn't count as a stroke. (Def. 31)

The Teeing Ground
The teeing ground is a rectangular area two club-lengths in depth. You may tee your ball anywhere in that rectangle. You're not required to stand in it. Teeing the ball back from the markers can sometimes give you a more level stance. (Def. 33)

provisional ball) from the teeing ground, the tee-markers are immovable obstructions (Definition 20).

This is the first time we run into a reference to "club-lengths" which occurs time and again within the Rules proper. The term is used instead of a specific distance, such as "six feet," because golfers aren't expected to carry tape measures. Any club is acceptable and, obviously, a driver is the best candidate, since it will make for the biggest rectangular area.

> In match play, the reckoning of holes is kept by the terms:
> —so many "holes up" or "all square," and so many "to play."
> A side is "dormie" when it is as many holes up as there are holes remaining to be played.

DEFINITION 34:

TERMS USED IN RECKONING IN MATCH PLAY

"Dormie" represents a curious case in which common and incorrect usage has virtually reversed the true meaning of a word. The player who is 6 holes up in match play with only 6 to play is the one who is dormie, not his opponent. The opponent might be said to be dormant.

> "Through the green" is the whole area of the course except:—
> a. Teeing ground and putting green of the hole being played;
> b. All hazards on the course.

DEFINITION 35:

THROUGH THE GREEN

The phrase "through the green" recurs throughout the Rules. It's a phrase that encompasses most of the course but *not* the tee of the hole being played, or the putting green of the hole being played, or any hazard. Everything else is "through the green." The distinctions are often critical. For example, if your ball is just off the green and there's casual water between your ball and the hole, you get no relief, i.e., you don't get to move it, since the ball is "through the green." But if the ball is on a putting green in the same circumstance, a special kind of relief is available under Rule 32.

> There are three recognized types of golf club:—
> An "iron" club is one with a head which usually is relatively narrow from face to back, and usually is made of steel.
> A "wood" club is one with a head relatively broad from face to back, and usually is made of wood, plastic or a light metal.
> A "putter" is a club designed primarily for use on the putting green—see Definition 25.

DEFINITION 36:

TYPES OF CLUB

37

3

THE RULES OF PLAY

RULE 1: THE GAME

The Game of Golf consists in playing a ball from the teeing ground into the hole by successive strokes in accordance with the Rules.

PENALTY FOR BREACH OF RULE:
Match play—Loss of hole; Stroke play—Disqualification.

The Rules of Golf begin with a straightforward definition of the game itself. One sentence of twenty-four words does the job.

This is the ideal place to begin to pick out the key words and phrases used in the Definitions and to become accustomed to the precise language used throughout the Rules. Note that there are no fewer than five check points in that sentence of twenty-four words:

*"Playing *a* ball" means playing *one* ball. You may not change to a shiny new ball once you reach the putting green.

*"The 'teeing ground,'" according to Definition 33, "is the starting place for the hole to be played." Definition 33 also specifies the dimensions of the teeing ground.

*"Into the hole" reveals that if you fail to hole out in stroke play, you're not playing this game.

*"By successive strokes" calls for an understanding of a stroke which, according to Definition 31, "is the forward movement of the club made with the intention of fairly striking at and moving the ball." Incidentally, Richard Peters came to play in the very first U.S. Amateur Championship in 1895 intending to putt with a billard cue. There is no such thing as a stroke made with a billiard cue because a billiard cue isn't a club.

*"In accordance with the Rules" is what this book is about. In order to understand and enjoy the game you have to know the Rules.

RULE 2: THE CLUB (DEF. 36) AND THE BALL

The United States Golf Association and the Royal and Ancient Golf Club of St. Andrews reserve the right to change the Rules and the interpretations regulating clubs and balls at any time.

The player's clubs, and the balls he uses, shall conform with Clauses 2 and 3 of this Rule.

a. GENERAL CHARACTERISTICS
The golf club shall be composed of a shaft and a head, and all of the various parts shall be fixed so that the club is one

(continued)

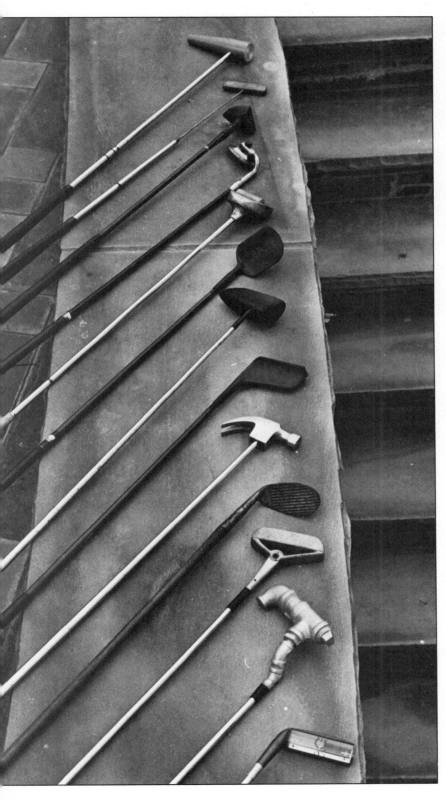

Illegal Clubs

Most of these clubs, for a variety of reasons, do not conform to the Rules of Golf. They're on display at the USGA Museum in Golf House, Far Hills, New Jersey. That piece of plumbing second from the bottom is actually a putter someone sent to Arnold Palmer with the thought that it might cure his problems on the greens. Arnold loaned it to the USGA. (R. 2-2)

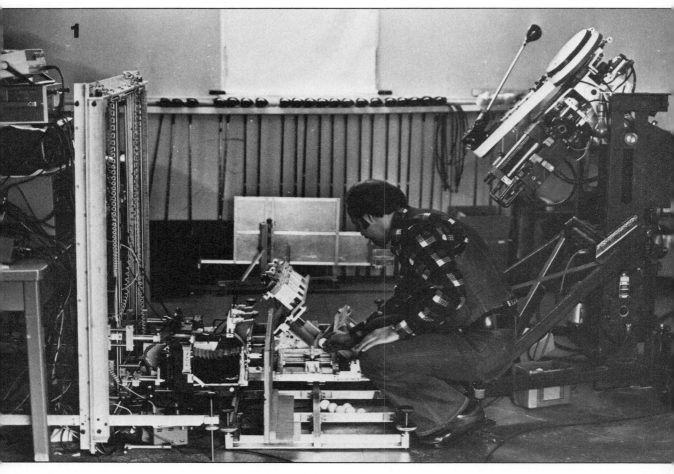

Iron Byron

There's no other machine like that of the USGA's mechanical golfer, which plays on a course all its own—a test range at USGA headquarters. The prototype was built to emulate the swing of my friend Byron Nelson. The USGA's Iron Byron is rigged with a laser beam and high-speed photo equipment. Every hit is dissected to the extent of a recording of the speed of the club at impact (in millionths of a second) and the wind velocity (horizontally and vertically) during the six seconds a ball is in flight. During the USGA's Overall Distance Standard tests a ball is placed on a tee (1) just after it's removed from an incubator where it was stored at 75 degrees Fahrenheit. A driver used in the Overall Distance Standard test is seen in the loaded position (2). The club is on the way down (3). When it strikes the ball it will be moving 109 miles per hour—approximately the club-head speed of a good player. If a ball carries and rolls more than 280 yards on the USGA range, it fails the test. The testing must be precise. Checks include a sheet of paper stretched in a frame ten yards in front of the tee (4). Calibration balls are first driven through the paper. If during a test round a ball tears the sheet by missing the hole, it's an indication something may be amiss. The technician is holding a small strip of tape that's applied on the "sweet spot" of the driver. If the mark made on the tape at impact moves outside a circle only 7/8 inch in diameter, that hit has not met the test specifications. (R. 2-3)

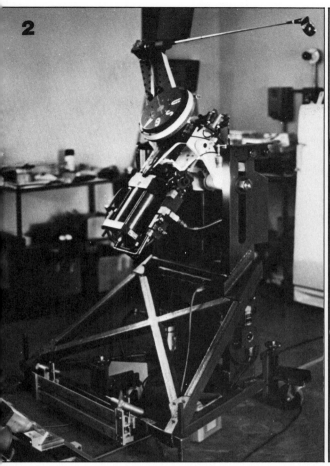

2

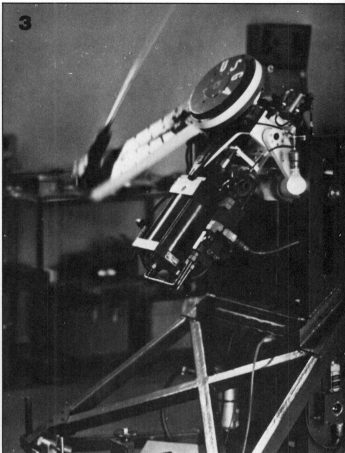

3

4

unit; the club shall not be designed to be adjustable, except for weight.

Note: *Playing characteristics not to be changed during a round—Rule 2-2b.*

The club shall not be substantially different from the traditional and customary form and make, and shall conform with the regulations governing the design of clubs at Appendix II and the specifications for markings on clubs at Appendix III.

b. PLAYING CHARACTERISTICS NOT TO BE CHANGED

The playing characteristics of a club shall not be purposely changed during a round; foreign material shall not be added to the club face at any time.

Note: *Players in doubt as to the legality of clubs are advised to consult the USGA. If a manufacturer is in doubt as to the legality of a club which he proposes to manufacture, he should submit a sample to the USGA for a ruling, such sample to become the property of the USGA for reference purposes.*

RULE 2-3:
THE BALL

a. SPECIFICATIONS

The weight of the ball shall be *not greater* than 1.620 ounces avoirdupois, and the size *not less* than 1.680 inches in diameter.

The velocity of the ball shall be not greater than 250 feet per second when measured on apparatus approved by the USGA: a maximum tolerance of 2% will be allowed. The temperature of the ball when so tested shall be 75 degrees Fahrenheit.

A brand of golf ball, when tested on apparatus approved by the USGA on the outdoor range at the USGA Headquarters under the conditions set forth in the Overall Distance Standard for golf balls on file with the USGA, shall not cover an average distance in carry and roll exceeding 280 yards, plus a tolerance of 8%. (Note: The 8% tolerance will be reduced to a minimum of 4% as test techniques are improved.)

Exception:—In international team competitions, the size of the ball shall be *not less* than 1.620 inches in diameter and the Overall Distance Standard shall not apply.

Note: *The Rules of the Royal and Ancient Golf Club of St. Andrews, Scotland, provide that the weight of the ball shall be not greater than 1.620 ounces avoirdupois, the size not less than 1.620 inches in diameter and the velocity not greater than 250 feet per second (with 2% tolerance) when measured on apparatus approved by the Royal and Ancient Golf Club.*

b. FOREIGN MATERIAL PROHIBITED

Foreign material shall not be applied to a ball for the purpose of changing its playing characteristics.

PENALTY FOR BREACH OF RULE: *Disqualification.*

Rule 2 exists in order to preserve the challenge of the game. Without reasonable standards, technology could create new kinds of clubs and balls that would change the very nature of the game. An armaments race in golf makes no sense at all.

The USGA's annual budget for equipment testing and research is nearly half a million dollars. It is money well spent.

On a world-wide basis the size of the ball is the only difference in the Rules of Golf. In Great Britain and other countries adhering to the Rules of the Royal and Ancient Golf Club of St. Andrews, the ball may be as small as 1.62 inches in diameter, compared to our minimum diameter of 1.68 inches.

The 6/100 of an inch can make quite a difference. I used the small ball while winning a tournament in Japan in 1976. I could have used either ball in that event but settled on the small one because it makes the game easier. The 1.62 ball goes farther (about 5 percent for me), it minimizes hooks and slices, and it bores into the wind better, but it is harder to maneuver.

The small ball shows up occasionally in this country. The penalty for using it is properly severe—disqualification—since the user has an advantage equivalent to teeing up many yards ahead of the tee markers.

The prohibitions against applying "foreign material" to the club face and to the ball are reactions against imaginative golfers who applied materials such as chalk or Vaseline in order, they claimed, to get more distance or to keep the ball on a straighter line by reducing spin. When I played on the Stanford University golf team, teammate Sandy Adelman spit on the face of his driver on every tee. That was before the USGA issued Rules of Golf Decision 72-39 on the very point. Sandy Adelman might not agree, but the USGA insists that "saliva is considered foreign material."

RULE 3: MAXIMUM OF FOURTEEN CLUBS

RULE 3-1:

SELECTION AND REPLACEMENT OF CLUBS

The player shall start a stipulated round with not more than fourteen clubs. He is limited to the clubs thus selected for that round except that, without unduly delaying play, he may:—

a. If he started with fewer than fourteen, add as many as will bring his total to that number;

b. Replace, with any club, a club which becomes unfit for play in the normal course of play.

The addition or replacement of a club or clubs may not be made by borrowing from any other person playing on the course.

RULE 3-2:

SIDE MAY SHARE CLUBS

Partners may share clubs provided that the total number of clubs carried by the side does not exceed fourteen.

(continued)

PENALTY FOR BREACH OF RULE 3-1 OR 3-2, REGARDLESS OF NUMBER OF WRONG CLUBS CARRIED:

Match play—Loss of one hole for each hole at which any violation occurred; maximum penalty per round: loss of two holes. The penalty shall be applied to the state of the match at the conclusion of the hole at which the violation is discovered, provided all players in the match have not left the putting green of the last hole of the match.

Bogey and Par Competitions—Penalties as in Match play.

Stroke play—Two strokes for each hole at which any violation occurred; maximum penalty per round: four strokes.

Stableford Competitions—From total points scored for the round, deduction of two points for each hole at which any violation occurred; maximum deduction per round: four points.

Note: *A serious breach of this Rule should be dealt with by the Committee under Rule 1.*

RULE 3-3:
WRONG CLUB DECLARED OUT OF PLAY

Any club carried or used in violation of this Rule shall be declared out of play by the player immediately upon discovery and thereafter shall not be used by the player during the round under *penalty of disqualification.*

There was no limit on the number of clubs until 1938. The ceiling was established because some players had gone to extremes in terms of carrying "specialty" clubs, supposedly designed to fit every kind of shot. Golf bags were becoming arsenals. Lawson Little and Craig Wood, two of the stars of the 1930s, went forth to battle with twenty-five clubs each. On the other hand, when Francis Ouimet won the 1913 U.S. Open, his ten-year-old caddie carried only seven clubs.

The number fourteen was selected by the USGA as the maximum because it corresponded to what was generally thought to be a standard set of clubs. Today most touring pros, including myself, carry irons numbered 1 through 9, pitching and sand wedges, a putter and only two woods.

Applying penalties for violations of Rule 3-1 can be tricky. Suppose in a match player A is 2 up against B after sixteen holes. They discover on the 17th tee that A has been carrying fifteen clubs. The status of the match immediately becomes even, since A gets the maximum penalty—loss of two holes.

Another example: A wins the first hole of a match against B, who then finds he's got an extra club. Poor B goes from 1 down to 2 down even though he's only played one hole, since the penalty is applied to the status of the match at the conclusion of the hole. (Incidentally, they don't skip the second hole; the match resumes on the second tee with the penalty added.)

There have been inadvertent and odd violations on Rule 3-1 on the tour. I was paired with Johnny Miller in the first round of the 1976 World Series of Golf when he suffered the maximum penalty of four strokes. As we were playing the 18th hole, Johnny noticed a tiny club in the bottom of his bag. It was an old Bull's-Eye putter he had modified for his son. In fact, it was nothing but grip and head, about 18 inches long. Nevertheless it *was* a golf club and it changed Johnny's 72 into a 76. Unfair? No! As a matter of fact, I often play with a friend who crouches over a putter not much longer than the one Johnny cut down for his son.

Just about every player I know has carried an extra club or more at some time. It happened to me once—in a qualifying round for the Missouri Amateur Championship in 1965. I managed to go out with eighteen clubs. At that time the penalty called for a maximum of four penalty strokes for every extra club. My 76 was converted into a nifty 92. That's the last time I or my caddie forgot to count my clubs before starting a round.

The penalty for an extra club was applied once even to Jack Nicklaus, who is a paragon when it comes to being meticulous. It happened this way: Jack and David Graham, who use the same brand of irons, were examining and discussing each other's clubs at a practice putting green. David's pitching wedge somehow found its way into Jack's bag. Jack made the discovery on the first hole.

Rule 3-1 limits you to the fourteen clubs you start with unless a club "becomes unfit for play in the normal course of play." When a shaft breaks as you're playing a stroke, you are entitled to a substitute. On the other hand, snapping a putter over your knee is *not* considered being "in the normal course of play."

The exposition of penalties following Rule 3-2 includes references to Bogey, Par and Stableford competitions—forms of play unfamiliar to many golfers. They'll be explained in Rule 39.

RULE 4: AGREEMENT TO WAIVE RULES PROHIBITED

> Players shall not agree to exclude the operation of any Rule or Local Rule or to waive any penalty incurred.
> PENALTY FOR BREACH OF RULE:
> *Match play—Disqualification of both sides;*
> *Stroke play—Disqualification of competitors concerned.*

Rule 4 expresses the principle that golf is meant to be the same game for everyone, with the same code of Rules, and the same set of penalties. It becomes a different game when opponents agree that they'll concede each other every putt "within the leather." They've made an agreement to ignore Rule 1 and *both* should be disqualified.

Rule 4 is vital to the integrity of the game, so the USGA's interpretations have been consistently and properly strict. Key decisions:

● In a match player A, who won the last hole, says to B, "You hit first. I don't want the honor." B agrees and plays first. Result: They've agreed to waive Rule 12-1, which provides that the last player who won a hole is to play first on every hole until he loses one, and both are to be disqualified. (76-13)

● A naughty thing happened in an event of the Cleveland Women's Golf Association: During a stroke-play round a competitor failed to hole out on a hole but continued to play the round. Her marker (another competitor in the same pairing) observed the violation but signed the score card anyway. Both were well aware of the violation. Result: Failing to hole out in stroke play is a violation of Rule 1 calling for disqualification. In this case *both* are disqualified on the basis that they agreed to waive Rule 1. (62-10)

RULE 5: GENERAL PENALTY

> Except when otherwise provided for, the penalty for a breach of a Rule or Local Rule is:
> *Match play—Loss of hole;*
> *Stroke play—Two strokes.*

Rule 5 is golf's version of Catch-22. It's especially useful when a Committee proclaims a Local Rule but then forgets to specify a penalty, such as when signs are posted near the first tee with messages like "Carts May Not Be Used in This Tournament" or "No Practice Putting after You've Holed Out." But that's all. No penalty is cited. Then, when the Committee, which has been lax, learns that someone has indeed ridden in a cart, the General Penalty can be applied and all arguments should cease.

RULE 6: MATCH PLAY

RULE 6-1:

WINNER OF HOLE

> In match play the game is played by holes.
> Except as otherwise provided for in the Rules, a hole is won by the side which holes its ball in the fewer strokes. In a handicap match the lower net score wins the hole.

RULE 6-2:

HALVED HOLE

> A hole is halved if each side holes out in the same number of strokes.
> When a player has holed out and his opponent has been left with a stroke for the half, nothing that the player who has holed out can do shall deprive him of the half which he has already gained; but if the player thereafter incur any penalty, the hole is halved.

RULE 6-3:

WINNER OF MATCH

> A match (which consists of a stipulated round, unless otherwise decreed by the Committee) is won by the side which is leading by a number of holes greater than the number of holes remaining to be played.

One of golf's special appeals is that it can be played two ways. The outcome can be determined on the basis either of holes won—*match play*—or of total number of strokes—*stroke play*. Arguments about the more valid form of play go on endlessly. I prefer stroke play, but I do not quarrel with the contention that match play (which is the only way golf was played for hundreds of years) is fascinating, calls for a different strategic approach and is, above all, intensely personal.

Rule 6 defines match play. It shouldn't cause you any trouble— except for, possibly, the second paragraph of Rule 6-2. There can be occasions when, for example, player A has holed out in 4 and his opponent is left with a putt for a 4. Player A then violates a Rule— let's say he inadvertently moves the opponent's ball. That violation calls for a one-stroke penalty, which is not assessed in this instance. Since the best his opponent could possibly do was make the putt and tie the hole, Rule 6-2 logically asserts that the hole is halved.

What about the phrase "stipulated round" in Rule 6-3? Again the Definitions are critical. The "stipulated round" requires that the holes be played in the correct sequence. In USGA Decision 76-2, prompted by Leon Lym, San Francisco, after six holes, two players got lost somehow and proceeded to play three holes other than the 7th, 8th and 9th. They then discovered the error and asked what they should do next. The answer was: Ignore the results of the three holes played out of sequence and go back and resume the match on the 7th hole, replaying the holes played in error, when they are reached.

RULE 7: STROKE PLAY

> The competitor who holes the stipulated round or rounds in the fewest strokes is the winner.

> If a competitor fail to hole out at any hole before he has played a stroke from the next teeing ground, or, in the case of the last hole of the round, before he has left the putting green, *he shall be disqualified. (Ball purposely moved, touched or lifted—Rules 27-1c and 35-1k.)*

Stroke play is commonly called "medal play"—a term that derives from the old British custom of playing occasional one-day competitions for the prize of a medal. Until the eighteenth century, when golf was already hundreds of years old, the game was always played at match play. Stroke play was inspired by the need for a means of completing a tournament in only one day.

Match play, however, was still considered *the* way the game should be played, when the USGA established its championships in 1895. The first U.S. Amateur was at match play, and the Open was tagged on almost as an afterthought the next day at stroke play (thirty-six holes in one day so the ten pros who entered wouldn't be away too long from their shops).

A classic application of Rule 7 occurred on the final hole of the playoff for the 1962 U.S. Open at Oakmont, near Pittsburgh. Twenty-one-year-old Jack Nicklaus, a rookie pro, had only to make a putt of three feet for a 71. Jack had marked the position of his ball with a coin. Meanwhile, Arnold Palmer was lining up a longer putt, which he made for a 74. He then graciously picked up Jack's coin as an act of concession. The former USGA Executive Director, Joseph C. Dey, Jr., immediately ordered Jack to replace the coin and hole out. You see, there is no such animal in stroke play as a concession. Technically, if Jack had walked off the 18th green without holing out, he could have been disqualified.

The parenthetical phrase at the end of Rule 7-2 is one of many like it, scattered throughout the Rules, to steer you in the right direction. Imagine that a player, his caddie or his partner blacks out and picks up the player's ball *before* it's holed out. Rule 7-2 says the ultimate penalty of disqualification is to be applied for failure to hole out. So we find the player standing there, ball in hand, knowing something awful has happened but not knowing what to do next. He wants desperately to hole out. Look, the book says, to Rules 27-1c and 35-1k for guidance. When you do, you learn that the ball must be replaced (not dropped) and that the penalty is one stroke.

RULE 8: PRACTICE

RULE 8-1:

DURING PLAY OF HOLE

During the play of a hole, a player shall not play any practice stroke.
Penalty for breach of Rule 8-1:
Match play—Loss of hole; Stroke play—Two strokes.

RULE 8-2:

BETWEEN HOLES

Between the play of two holes, a player shall not play a practice stroke from any hazard, or on or to a putting green other than that of the hole last played.
Penalty for breach of Rule 8-2:
*Match play—Loss of hole; Stroke play—Two strokes.
*The penalty applies to the next hole.

RULE 8-3:

STROKE PLAY

On any day of a stroke competition or play-off, a competitor shall not practice on the competition course before a round or play-off. When a competition extends over consecutive days, practice on the competition course between rounds is prohibited.

If a competition extending over consecutive days is to be played on more than one course, practice between rounds on any competition course remaining to be played is prohibited.

Note: *The Committee may, at its discretion, waive or modify these prohibitions in the conditions of the competition (Appendix 1-12).*
Penalty for breach of Rule 8-3: *Disqualification.*
(Duty of Committee to define practice ground—Rule 36-4b.)
Note 1: *A practice swing is not a practice stroke and may be taken at any place on the course provided the player does*
(continued)

not violate the Rules.

Note 2: *Unless otherwise decided by the Committee, there is no penalty for practice on the course on any day of a match play competition.*

The language of Rule 8 is finicky, and well it might be, since golf is intended to be an exercise in finite judgments and muscle memory skills. If you could rehearse each shot before playing it, golf would be a different game. I've averaged a fraction more than 70 strokes a round on the tour in recent years. If the Rules allowed me to rehearse each shot one time before it counted, I think I could reduce that average to 66.

Rule 8-2 is framed so as to allow for such innocuous acts as chipping near a tee when you're delayed. It also permits you to practice putt on the hole you've just completed—assuming you can do so *without delaying play.* On the pro tour, practice putting is prohibited by a Local Rule because if permitted, it might retard play. Too, all that extra traffic in the critical area near the hole would roughen the surface to the detriment of those who have late starting times.

The application of the penalty for a violation of Rule 8-2 is curious. Suppose a player replays a bunker shot on the 4th hole, which he's just won in a match. A clear-cut violation, since he's played a practice stroke in a hazard, but which hole does he lose? The penalty applies to the *next hole,* which means that he and his opponent skip hole 5 entirely and proceed directly to the 6th tee.

The restrictions against practicing on the course in stroke play are stringent. Rule 8-3 keeps us from surging onto the course as soon as the holes are cut for a round and from thoroughly familiarizing ourselves with every little break and roll near that day's holes.

Watch out for Rule 8-3 when you're involved in a 36-hole stroke-play qualifying event over a weekend. You may play the first round Saturday morning and decide to go out on the course Saturday afternoon for some practice. Don't! The penalty is disqualification unless the Committee specifically has said otherwise.

The Rules of Golf Committee is often forced to find its way through thickets of technicalities in interpreting the Rules. Here are a couple of examples under the practice category:

● Robert W. Ferguson wrote about a "character" at the Wheeling Country Club, Wheeling, West Virginia, who, before making his "regular shot," habitually tossed down plastic balls and hit them in the direction of the hole. His opponents complained bitterly. The player said swatting at plastic balls was not covered in the Rules of Golf. The USGA ruled that the player was, in fact, playing practice strokes and violating Rule 8-1. (55-17)

● A letter from Sandy Armour, of Delray Beach, Florida, described a driving range adjacent to a fairway, and a woman, after playing her second shot to the green, flicked a ball with a red band painted on it back to where it belonged on a practice range. This was a stroke-play happening, and the Committee socked her with two strokes. She took her case to the USGA, which ordained that "casually flicking a range ball, apparently only for the purpose of tidying up the course, should not be considered a violation." The Decision carefully pointed out that "under some circumstances," hitting a range ball back to the range would be a violation, e.g., the next shot calls for a carry of 190 yards over water, and the player carefully addresses a range ball with a 3 wood and bashes it back toward the practice tee. (64-1)

RULE 9: ADVICE (DEF. 2) AND ASSISTANCE

RULE 9-1:

GIVING OR ASKING FOR ADVICE; RECEIVING ASSISTANCE

a. ADVICE
A player may give advice to, or ask for advice from, only his partner or either of their caddies.
b. ASSISTANCE
In making a stroke, a player shall not seek or accept physical assistance or protection from the elements.

RULE 9-2:

INDICATING LINE OF PLAY

Except on the putting green, a player may have the line of play indicated to him by anyone, but no one shall stand on or close to the line while the stroke is being played. Any mark placed during the play of a hole by the player or with his knowledge to indicate the line shall be removed before the stroke is played.
(Indicating line of play on putting green—Rule 35-1e.)
PENALTY FOR BREACH OF RULE:
Match play—Loss of hole; Stroke play—Two strokes.

There's no surer nor more painful way to learn a Rule than to be penalized once for breaking it. I learned all about "advice" during the 1968 Amateur Championship at the Scioto Country Club in Columbus, Ohio. Although I was only seventeen, I had played enough golf by then to know better. I was paired with Mike Taylor, another young amateur, from Mississippi. We hit it off well and began to help each other by telling what clubs we used. On one hole I yelled clear across a fairway to Mike to ask him what he'd hit and Mike answered. USGA official Pete Tufts could hardly believe his ears. Mike and I were each penalized two strokes—I for asking for advice, and Mike for giving it.

A golfer may, of course, ask his caddie for advice. He can also seek help from his partner or his partner's caddie. A partner, remember, is someone on your side. Mike Taylor was *not* my "partner"; we were "fellow-competitors."

The USGA has been forced to split some very fine hairs in making interpretations of "advice." Asking an opponent or fellow-competitor to name the club he has used is forbidden, but it's not a violation if you look into his bag to discover which club is missing. On the other hand, if your opponent or fellow-competitor should go to the extreme of draping a towel over his clubs to maintain secrecy, you are not allowed to strip the towel. Decision 73-30 says so. (As a practical matter, if I'm close to another player, I can identify the club he's selected by the club face 99 percent of the time).

Brave the Elements
The Rules do not *permit a player to be shielded from the elements in the act of making a stroke. (R. 9-1b)*

Indicating Line of Play
My caddie, or anyone else for that matter, can show me the line (top) to the hole, but he isn't allowed to stand on or near the line while the stroke is being played. He has moved off the line in the bottom picture. (R. 9-2)

The Rules-makers have also had to agonize over the modern vogue for playing the game by yardage numbers. I know how far from the hole I am before I play almost every shot, and I also know the relative location of the hole on the green, which is expressed, for example, as 6 paces from the front and 5 paces from the right, according to a sheet produced by tour officials and distributed to our caddies each day of a tournament.

Given this availability of precise yardage data, what should happen under the Rules when a player asks another about yardage or the location of the hole, whether or not printed charts are available? Is that asking for "advice" or isn't it? The USGA has taken what seems to me the very pragmatic and sensible stand that distance from a *landmark* (a tree, bunker, sprinkler head) to the middle of the green is an ascertainable fact, that the location of a hole is a matter of "public information" and that neither comes under the heading of "counsel nor suggestion," which are defined as advice in Definition 2. On the other hand, if you ask another player the distance to the hole from a nonpermanent object, such as a ball, you've asked for a kind of advice.

A piece of obscure but interesting history: The practice of charting courses by yards in terms of reference points ("123 yards from front of fairway bunker on right to middle of green") was the product of the nimble mind of Gene Andrews, a fine amateur from Southern California. Andrews first charted a treeless links course in Great Britain during a practice round before a British Amateur during the 1950s because he found that the barren land gave him no sense of where he was in terms of distance to the hole. Andrews continued the practice at home. Deane Beman picked it up from Gene during the 1958 U.S. Amateur Championship and passed it along to his good friend Jack Nicklaus. It wasn't very long before the televised image of Nicklaus peering at his yardage notes in fairways aroused the curiosity of golfers everywhere.

As for Rule 9-1b, the only physical assistance I can imagine would be to have someone hold me steady as I took a precarious stance on a steep slope. Even your caddie is not allowed to hold on to you. Protection from the elements, however, is something we could all use when a high wind causes rain to slant and penetrate to the skin. Without this restriction you'd see caddies shielding their players from the elements with huge umbrellas.

Rule 9-2 is simple enough. It means that when you can't see what you're aiming at, anyone can help you out by indicating the line to the target, but before you play the stroke, your helper has to get off that line.

Some landmark interpretations of Rule 9:

● A player on the Loras College team of Dubuque, Iowa, had a delicate 40-yard pitch shot to execute. He approved and watched with great interest as a teammate, at that point a spectator following the match, dropped a ball and played the shot. The opponents from Loyola College of Illinois protested vehemently. The Loras player, who may well have benefited from his teammate's action, should have been disqualified from that hole. (54-8)

● A player wants to take a lesson between rounds of a 36-hole match for the club championship of the Eugene (Oregon) Country Club. That's OK, because the proscription against receiving advice applies only *during* the stipulated round, which consists of 18 holes. As a matter of fact, Jerry Pate skipped lunch between rounds of the final match of the 1974 U.S. Amateur, which he won, in order to take a lesson from his college coach, Conrad Rehling. (64-27)

● A double caddie often finds himself in a delicate position. Player A asks their caddie what club player B, his opponent, just hit. It's no violation, because Definition 7 told us that a double caddie "is always deemed to be the caddie of the player whose ball is involved." Since it was his ball that was involved, player A was entitled to attempt to pry loose any useful information the caddie possessed. (73-4)

RULE 10: INFORMATION AS TO STROKES TAKEN

RULE 10-1:
GENERAL

The number of strokes a player has taken shall include any penalty strokes incurred.

RULE 10-2:
MATCH PLAY

A player who has incurred a penalty shall inform his opponent as soon as possible. If he fail to do so, he shall be deemed to have given wrong information.

An opponent is entitled to ascertain from the player, during the play of a hole, the number of strokes he has taken and, after play of a hole, the number of strokes taken on the hole just completed.

If during the play of a hole the player give or be deemed to give wrong information as to the number of strokes taken, he shall incur no penalty if he correct the mistake before his opponent has played his next stroke. If after play of a hole the player give or be deemed to give wrong information as to the number of strokes taken on the hole just completed, he shall incur no penalty if he correct his mistake before any player plays from the next teeing ground or, in the case of the last hole of the match, before all players leave the putting green. If the player fail so to correct the wrong information, *he shall lose the hole.*

RULE 10-3:
STROKE PLAY

A competitor who has incurred a penalty should inform his marker as soon as possible.

Rule 10 doesn't cause a stir in stroke play, since it all comes out in the wash at the end of a round when we check our cards, hole by hole. Rule 10-3 says that in stroke play a competitor should tell his marker of any penalties as soon as possible, but the difference between the conditional "should" and the absolute "shall" means that a competitor whose ball moves after he's taken his stance and addressed it need not announce that doleful fact to the marker, fifty yards on the other side of the fairway, with a shout of rage. It can be done later.

In match play, however, it is the essence of the game that opponents know how they stand at all times. If your opponent lies 3 in a bunker near the green, and you lie 1 only 125 yards from the hole, your next stroke is likely to be properly cautious. But if you *think* he lies 2 because you don't know he incurred a penalty stroke along the way, you may be misled into flirting with the bunker yourself.

The word "deemed" in Rule 10-2 gives some readers pause. In this context, it means that a failure to announce that you've incurred a penalty is just the same as being asked how many strokes you've taken and coming up with the wrong answer.

Confusion about scores in four-ball play caused these interesting cases to be considered:

● From Bob Bodington of the Hartford Golf Club in West Hartford, Connecticut: A and B, partners, both lie 4. C, an opponent, holes a putt. A asks, "Is that 4 in?" And C replies, "Yes." A and B pick up, believing they've lost the hole. Then C says, "Oh, no, I made a 5."

Under Rule 10-2, C and D would ordinarily lose the hole, since one of them gave wrong information, but in this case Rule 6-2 becomes operative, and the hole is automatically halved, since the best that A and B could have done was tie C's 5. (61-27)

● It's A and B against C and D again, as told by Jack Rowland, of New York City. During a hole D tells A he has taken two strokes. Before the hole is completed, D reveals he had taken three strokes at the time he was asked.

Result: C and D lose the hole, i.e., the penalty applies to the *side* and not just to the player who gave the wrong information. (63–18)

RULE 11: DISPUTES, DECISIONS AND DOUBT AS TO RIGHTS

RULE 11-1:

CLAIMS AND PENALTIES

a. MATCH PLAY
In match play, if a dispute or doubt arise between the players on any point, in order that a claim may be considered it must be made before any player in the match plays from the next teeing ground or, in the case of the last hole of the match, before all players in the match leave the putting green. No later claim shall be considered unless it is based on facts previously unknown to the player making the claim and the player making the claim had been given wrong information (Rule 10) by an opponent. In any case, however, no later claim shall be considered after the result of the match has been officially announced, unless the Committee is satisfied that the opponent knew he was giving wrong information.

b. STROKE PLAY
In stroke play, no penalty shall be imposed after the competition is closed unless the Committee is satisfied that the competitor has knowingly returned a score for any hole lower than actually taken (Rule 38-3); no penalty shall be rescinded after the competition is closed. A competition is

(continued)

deemed to have closed:—

In stroke play only—When the result of the competition is officially announced.

In stroke play qualifying followed by match play—When the player has teed off in his first match.

RULE 11-2:
REFEREE'S DECISION

If a referee has been appointed by the Committee, his decision shall be final.

RULE 11-3:
COMMITTEE'S DECISION

In the absence of a referee, the players shall refer any dispute to the Committee, whose decision shall be final.

If the Committee cannot come to a decision, it shall refer the dispute to the USGA Rules of Golf Committee whose decision shall be final.

If the point in dispute or doubt has not been referred to the Rules of Golf Committee, the player or players have the right to refer an agreed statement through the Secretary of the Club to the Rules of Golf Committee for an opinion as to the correctness of the decision given. The reply will be sent to the Secretary of the Club or Clubs concerned.

If play be conducted other than in accordance with the Rules of Golf, the Rules of Golf Committee will not give a decision on any question.

RULE 11-4:
DECISION BY EQUITY

If any point in dispute be not covered by the Rules or Local Rules, the decision shall be made in accordance with equity.

RULE 11-5:
STROKE PLAY: DOUBT AS TO PROCEDURE

In stroke play only, when during play of a hole a competitor is doubtful of his rights or procedure, he may, without penalty, play a second ball. After the doubtful situation has arisen and before taking further action, he should announce to his marker his decision to proceed under this Rule and which ball he will score with if the Rules permit.

On completing the round, the competitor must report the facts immediately to the Committee; if he fail to do so, *he shall be disqualified.* If the Rules allow the procedure selected in advance by the competitor, the score with the ball selected shall be his score for the hole. Should the competitor fail to announce in advance his procedure or selection, the ball with the higher score shall count if the Rules allow the procedure adopted for such ball.

Note 1: *A second ball played under Rule 11-5 is not a provisional ball under Rule 30.*

Note 2: *The privilege of playing a second ball does not exist in match play.*

Rule 11 covers the hypersensitive area of doubts and disagreements and tells how to settle them. The 1980 version of Rule 11 was revised extensively. Each of its sections deserves careful consideration.

1a—Focus on "claim" and on "wrong information."

A claim, while there are nice and not-so-nice ways of going about it, boils down to telling your opponent that you think he has violated a Rule. In order for a claim to be valid, it must be *timely*. It's no good watching him ground his club in a hazard on the 12th hole and bringing up the painful subject when you're 1 down playing the 18th. You see, the statute of limitations for the 12th hole—given that you know all the facts—expired when one of you drove from the 13th tee.

Wrong information usually has to do with the number of strokes taken. It applies to a bold-faced lie (having taken seven strokes but saying you've only taken six), and in an application that goes right to the heart of the game, it also applies to a failure to call a penalty on yourself.

Some landmark 11-1a Decisions:

● A pushed his tee shot into the rough and among trees on the 8th hole. After searching for three or four minutes, he found a ball on the adjoining 9th fairway. It was the same make and number as his ball. A went on to win the 8th hole. After they began to play the 9th hole, a player in the group ahead of them informed A that he had played the wrong ball on the 8th hole. After examining the ball again, A conceded that he had indeed played a wrong ball. Could B claim the 8th hole retroactively? Yes, he could. A had given wrong information by failing to inform his opponent of the violation, even though A was not aware he had played a wrong ball. This would apply anytime until the result of the match was officially announced —in club play that means when the winner's name is posted on a scoresheet. (61-5)

● Bernard Boles, of Buffalo, New York, wanted a mix-up resolved: With his opponent B safely on in 2, A takes three strokes to get out of a bunker and concedes the hole. As B picks up his ball, he realizes and announces that he played a wrong ball during the play of the hole. A, although he has conceded, claims the hole.

A's claim is valid, since it was made before either player played from the next tee. He wins the hole. (59-25)

● James Robertson, golf coach at Ramsey (New Jersey) High School, asked if a player calling a violation on a hole has to cite the Rule violated or if it is good enough that he knows that *some* Rule has been violated.

The claim must be reasonably specific and accurate, but the player calling the hole doesn't have to know its number. For instance, if A putts straddle or croquet style and B says, "The Rules prohibit such a stance and I call the hole," the Committee should uphold the claim. But if B had said, "I call the hole because you pushed the ball instead of stroking it," the claim should not be upheld, since a saddle-style stroke is not a push. (70-6)

11-1b—On the morning after the 1977 Jackie Gleason Inverrary Classic ended, Hale Irwin was jolted by a newspaper account of the final round. He read that Grier Jones had been penalized for dropping into a special "ball drop" area after hitting his ball into a water hazard. The Local Rule that applied to the situation said the drop area could be used only if a ball entered the hazard in a particular area. Jones had misunderstood the Rule and used the drop area, even though he was not entitled to use it. Irwin realized he had done exactly the same thing. He had failed to include a two-stroke penalty on the hole in question, he had turned in a score lower than the one he actually made and he should be disqualified. He had tied for seventh and his prize was $7,375.

Irwin called Clyde Mangum, Deputy Commissioner of Tour Operations, and, in effect, turned himself in. He told Mangum of his error and said he considered himself disqualified and would return his check forthwith. Mangum replied that Irwin could not be penalized after the results of the tournament had been announced, since wrong information had not been given. He hadn't knowingly violated a Rule. Irwin was adamant. Mangum said he would not accept the check, and suggested that they call the USGA Executive Director P. J. Boatwright, who, as Mangum knew he would, told Irwin that it would be contrary to the Rules of Golf for any penalty to be invoked at that point.

If the incident had occurred between rounds while the tournament was still in progress, Irwin would have been disqualified under Rule 38-3, for returning a score lower than he'd actually made. The point behind this Rule is that there *must* be a time when a competition is final. Irwin happened to learn of the violation the day after it happened, but he might just as easily have learned of it on a practice putting green with Grier Jones six months later. Without a statute of limitations we'd never be certain of the outcome of a tournament.

11-2—The only time I play with a referee is when I happen to be in contention in the last rounds of either the U.S. or British Open Championship or the PGA Championship. Then, referees are customarily appointed to accompany the final pairings. All my other competitive rounds are administered by representatives of the Committee (in my case the PGA Tour staff) sprinkled around the course and available to help when needed.

11-3—Dozens of times every year, written replies to Rules questions from the USGA begin with these ominous words: "The Committee's decision was wrong. However, it was final under Rule 11-3."

It has to be that way. Someone has to be in charge to make rulings on the spot, and sometimes that someone is going to make a mistake.

At least 99 percent of golf is played informally, and most of that 99 percent is played at match play. If there is a doubt or dispute about the Rules out on the course, the players should agree on the facts and then continue the match, even though they will not then be sure of the status of the match. They should get a decision as soon as they can without delaying play. Whoever is in charge of a golf course should authorize someone to make decisions, and it makes eminently good sense for that authority to be given to the golf professional.

11-4—It is impossible to cover everything in any set of Rules and therefore it is sometimes necessary to rule "in equity." Here's a sampling of USGA Decisions under Rule 11-4:

● This actually happened to Mrs. Vera Lake, of Shreveport, Louisiana. She took a hefty cut at a ball on an embankment. She couldn't find her ball at first but then saw it stuck to the face of the club held firmly by wet clay.

Answer: Mrs. Lake should drop the ball as near as possible to the spot where the club was when the ball lodged on it. No penalty but, naturally, the stroke Mrs. Lake made was counted. (53-2)

● As a player putted at the Montgomery Country Club, Montgomery, Alabama, his caddie pulled the flagstick. The cup-liner came up with the flagstick. The ball hit the cup-liner.

Answer: The cup should have been restored to its original position and the ball played from where it then lay—one foot from the hole —without penalty. (60-49)

● Lynn Smith, of Pasadena, California, had fun with this one: As a player started into a bunker to play a shot, she noticed a rattlesnake near her ball. What to do?

Answer: It's not reasonable to expect a player to play from such a dangerous situation. The player is allowed to place a ball without penalty in the hazard, or in a similar nearby hazard, in a situation she does not regard as dangerous, as near as possible to the spot where the ball lay and in a lie similar to that which it originally occupied. The same applies to bees and wasps and, indeed, a similar ruling was made for players in a bunker infested by yellow jackets in the 1949 Amateur Championship at the Oak Hill Country Club, Rochester, New York. (67-2)

● A caddie for Lancy Smith, one of the best American women amateurs, accidentally kicks her opponent's ball marker closer to the hole.

Answer: The coin should be replaced as close as possible to the spot where it lay without penalty to anyone. A ball marker is a movable obstruction and does not have the same status as a ball in play. (75-5)

11-5—The language of Rule 11-5 is straightforward and should not require clarification, since it was significantly improved in 1980. What needs to be emphasized is that the privilege of playing a second ball applies only in stroke play and not in match play. Why not in match play? The essence of match play is that players have a right to know the status of the match. The introduction of a second ball erodes that right. The vital element of strategy in match play goes out the window if a player has to play against two balls, not knowing which one counts.

RULE 12: THE HONOR (DEF. 16)

RULE 12-1:

THE HONOR

a. MATCH PLAY

A match begins by each side playing a ball from the first teeing ground in the order of the draw. In the absence of a draw, the option of taking the honor shall be decided by lot.

The side which wins a hole shall take the honor at the next teeing ground. If a hole has been halved, the side which had the honor at the previous teeing ground shall retain it.

b. STROKE PLAY

The honor shall be taken as in match play.

a. MATCH PLAY

If, on the teeing ground, a player play when his opponent should have played, the opponent may immediately require the player to abandon the ball so played and to play a ball in correct order, without penalty.

b. STROKE PLAY

If, on the teeing ground, a competitor by mistake play out of turn, no penalty shall be incurred and the ball shall be in play.

c. SECOND BALL FROM TEE

If a player play a second ball, including a provisional ball, from the tee, he should do so after the opponent or the fellow-competitor has played his first stroke. If a player play a second ball out of turn, the provisions of Clauses 2a and 2b of this Rule apply.

Everyday golf is played on a handicap basis and the honor is determined by the *net* scores of the preceding hole.

One of my favorite golf stories turns on a question of "The Honor." According to Joe Dey, the USGA granted a special exemption from qualifying for the 1941 U.S. Open to one Dr. Walter Ratto of Brazil for reasons that are still obscure. Dr. Ratto stepped to the first tee of the Colonial Country Club at Fort Worth and slammed his ball into a tree very near the tee. The ball caromed *behind* the tee. The young pro with whom Dr. Ratto was paired reviewed the situation carefully and then asked the doctor, "Is it now my honor or are you away?" (The pro should then have driven.)

RULE 13: PLAYING OUTSIDE TEEING GROUND (DEF. 33)

RULE 13-1:

MATCH PLAY

If a player, when starting a hole, play a ball from outside the teeing ground, the opponent may immediately require the player to replay the stroke, in which case the player shall tee a ball and play the stroke from within the teeing ground, without penalty.

RULE 13-2:

STROKE PLAY

If a competitor, when starting a hole, play from outside the teeing ground, *he shall be penalized two strokes* and shall then play from within the teeing ground. Strokes played by a competitor from outside the teeing ground do not count in his score. If the competitor fail to rectify his mistake before making a stroke on the next teeing ground or, in the case of the last hole of the round, before leaving the putting green, *he shall be disqualified.*

Note: STANCE. *A player may take his stance outside the teeing ground to play a ball within it.*

I've never known an instance when a golfer purposely teed his ball in front of the tee markers, but it certainly happens occasionally and usually because the markers have been installed carelessly so that a line drawn between the front of the markers would not form a right angle with the line of play.

A ball teed outside the teeing ground raises a nice question of ethics. In match play the opponent of the player whose ball is teed in the wrong place has every opportunity to use the Rules cruelly by requiring the shot to be replayed. That's not the way the game should be played. If I saw an opponent's ball teed ahead of the markers, I'd let him know about it, and I'd expect him to do the same for me. As a matter of fact, we handle it just that way on the tour.

Playing from outside the teeing ground in stroke play calls for a two-stroke penalty. Failure to correct the mistake before playing from the next tee results in disqualification. Suppose a player in stroke play plays from the wrong set of tee markers or is unfamiliar with the course and begins to play a hole out of sequence. Let's say he then plays a second stroke before the error is brought to his attention. Rule 13-2 says that he must return to the correct set of markers and play the hole correctly. The stroke he plays from the right markers is his *third* (not fifth), since the strokes he played starting at the wrong markers do not count and only the penalty strokes are added.

RULE 14: BALL FALLING OFF TEE

> If a ball, when not in play, fall off a tee or be knocked off a tee by the player in addressing it, it may be re-teed without penalty, but if a stroke be made at the ball in these circumstances, whether the ball be moving or not, the stroke shall be counted but no penalty shall be incurred.

Whenever a ball falls off or is nudged accidentally from a tee, some joker has to say "That's 1." It is *not* because the definition of a stroke told us that there is no stroke unless the club moves forward *and* the player intends to strike the ball. The ball is not in play until a stroke is made. Rule 14 is necessary only to resolve the question of whether or not the ball can be teed again and, of course, it can.

The atmosphere must have been electric in a club match reported by Mrs. Arnold Simensen, of Winchendon, Massachusetts. It led to Decision 53-46, which goes like this: A teed his ball, addressed it and then missed it completely. A whiff! Then, after he addressed the ball again, A nudged his ball from the tee. B said A was then shooting 3 and must play the ball where it lay even though it was still within the teeing ground. A vehemently claimed he could re-tee without penalty. Answer: Poor A did lay 2, since, according to Definition 5, his ball was in play as soon as he made a stroke on the teeing ground. Therefore, A's ball was in play as soon as he whiffed it and it was also in play when he accidentally moved it. Since he moved it after address, he had to play the ball as it lay, as required by Rule 27-1f.

I well remember John Mahaffey completing his stroke as his ball was toppling from the tee on a hole at the Firestone Country Club. John's driver barely made contact with the ball, which dribbled only a few yards off the tee and into a rotten lie. John, whose sense of humor is one of the tour's most redeeming features, later lamented what terrible luck he'd suffered in not missing the ball entirely. He could not have re-teed the ball, but at least it would still have been sitting up nicely in the teeing ground.

RULE 15: ORDER OF PLAY IN THREESOME OR FOURSOME

RULE 15-1:

GENERAL

> In a threesome or a foursome, the partners shall strike off alternately from the teeing grounds, and thereafter shall strike alternately during the play of each hole. Penalty strokes (Definition 24) do not affect the order of play.

RULE 15-2:

MATCH PLAY

> If a player play when his partner should have played, *his side shall lose the hole.* In a match comprising more than one stipulated round, the partners shall not change the order of striking from the teeing grounds after any stipulated round.

RULE 15-3:

STROKE PLAY

> If the partners play a stroke or strokes in incorrect order, such stroke or strokes shall be cancelled, and *the side shall be penalized two strokes.* A ball shall then be put in play as nearly as possible at the spot from which the side first played in incorrect order. This must be done before a stroke has been played from the next teeing ground, or, in the case of the last hole of the round, before the side has left the putting green. If they fail to do so, *they shall be disqualified.* If the first ball was played from the teeing ground, a ball may be teed anywhere within the teeing ground; if from through the green or a hazard, it shall be dropped; if on the putting green, it shall be placed.
>
> **Note:** *As in stroke play a stipulated round cannot be more than 18 holes (Def. 30), the order of play between partners may be changed for a second or subsequent round, unless the conditions of the competition provide otherwise.*

Rule 15 is almost never referred to, because a threesome is virtually an extinct form of play and we very seldom play foursomes in the United States.

Remember what Definition 28 said: A threesome is *not* what happens when three golfers play together; it's a form of play in which one plays against two, and each side plays one ball, i.e., the team of two plays alternate strokes; a foursome is *not* what happens when four golfers play together; it's a form of competition in which two

Nudged Off the Tee

*There's no penalty when a
ball falls or is knocked off
a tee before a stroke. The
ball may be teed again. The
stroke, remember, calls for
intent. (R. 14 and Def. 31)*

play against two with each side using one ball playing alternate strokes.

RULE 16: BALL PLAYED AS IT LIES; EMBEDDED BALL

RULE 16-1:

GENERAL

The ball shall be played as it lies, except as otherwise provided for in the Rules or Local Rules.
(Ball at Rest Moved by Player, Purposely—Rule 27-1c.)
(Ball at Rest Moved by Player, Accidentally—Rule 27-1d.)
(Ball at Rest Moving Accidentally after Address—Rule 27-1f.)

RULE 16-2:

EMBEDDED BALL

A ball embedded in its own pitch-mark in any closely mown area through the green may be lifted and dropped, without penalty, as near as possible to the spot where it lay but not nearer the hole.
PENALTY FOR BREACH OF RULE 16-2:
Match play—Loss of hole; Stroke Play—Two strokes.

"Play the ball as it lies" is an underlying principle of the Rules. The italicized phrases following Rule 16-1 were inserted to steer the reader from the general to the specific of Rule 27—or, rather, what to do when the ball is not played as it lies but is moved instead.

Rule 16-2 is an important 1980 innovation. Prior to 1980, relief from an embedded ball was granted *only* when a Committee invoked a Local Rule allowing for such relief. The Local Rule, however, was always in use at USGA competitions and on our professional tour. The purpose of Local Rules is to cover "abnormal" situations. Since giving relief without penalty from embedded balls seemed to be not only eminently fair but had become the accepted thing to do, the Rules-makers reasoned that the custom should be formalized.

The USGA says that "closely mown areas" means those cut at fairway height or less. Rule 16-2 does not allow relief for balls embedded in rough. If a Committee feels conditions warrant providing relief for more than "closely mown areas" it is necessary to invoke a Local Rule.

RULE 17: IMPROVING LIE OR STANCE AND INFLUENCING BALL PROHIBITED

RULE 17-1:

IMPROVING LINE OF PLAY OR LIE PROHIBITED

A player shall not improve, or allow to be improved, his line of play, the position or lie of his ball or the area of his intended swing by moving, bending or breaking anything fixed or growing, or by removing or pressing down sand, loose soil, cut turf placed in position or other irregularities

(continued)

Don't Improve the Lie
Here's an example of a blatant violation. The lie is being improved by pressing down behind the ball so that the ball sits up. One of the principles underlying the Rules is that you are to play the course as you find it. (R. 17-1)

of surface except:—

    a. As may occur in the course of fairly taking his stance;

    b. In making the stroke or the backward movement of his club for the stroke;

    c. On the teeing ground a player may create or eliminate irregularities of surface;

    d. In repairing damage to the putting green under Rule 35-1c.

The club may be grounded only lightly and must not be pressed on the ground.

(Sand and loose soil on the putting green—Def. 17 and Rule 35-1b.)

(Removal of obstructions—Rule 31-1.)

Note: *Things fixed include objects defining out of bounds.*

RULE 17-2:
LONG GRASS AND BUSHES

If a ball lie in long grass, rushes, bushes, whins, heather or the like, only so much thereof shall be touched as will enable the player to find and identify his ball; nothing shall be done which may in any way improve its lie.

The player is not of necessity entitled to see the ball when playing a stroke.

RULE 17-3:
BUILDING OF STANCE PROHIBITED

A player is always entitled to place his feet firmly on the ground when taking his stance, but he is not allowed to build a stance.

RULE 17-4:
EXERTING INFLUENCE ON BALL

No player or caddie shall take any action to influence the position or the movement of a ball except in accordance with the Rules.

PENALTY FOR BREACH OF RULE:

Match play—Loss of hole; Stroke play—Two strokes.

Note: *In the case of a serious breach of Rule 17-4, the Committee may impose a penalty of disqualification.*

It may well be that Rule 17 is violated more often than any other Rule. The impulse to make the stroke a little bit easier by moving anything bothersome or pressing down with the club head is powerful. Moreover, the application of this Rule often involves judgment rather than agreed-upon facts. This Rule is violated:

*When during a practice swing a branch or twig is snapped or some leaves are removed so that the actual stroke is easier to accomplish.

*Whenever a player presses firmly behind his ball (except on the teeing ground) so that the ball sits up a little better.

*When a player brushes aside sand or loose soil on his line that is not on a putting green.

*When a ball lies in shrubbery and the player gets to the ball like

THE RULES OF PLAY

a bull in a china shop by breaking or bending moving branches that bothered his stroke or were in his line and which he need *not* have disturbed in order to take a fair stance.

*By pushing aside long grass which covers his ball. The best way to describe what is meant by "fairly taking a stance" is to cite the answer given in Decision 52-9, in reply to C.R.L. Crenshaw, of Los Angeles:

The basic object of Rule 17-1 is to prohibit improving the position of the ball.

In the course of taking a reasonable stance, for example, the player might bend growing objects, such as tall grass, and as a consequence the line of play might be affected. The Rule excuses this provided it occurs as an incident in the course of taking the stance.

The player is entitled to take his stance fairly. The word "fairly" should be read in a normal sense. To put it in other words, the player may take a stance which is as reasonable as could be expected in the light of the ball's situation. This is no guarantee that he is to have a perfect stance; if that were so, the Rules might permit players to carry axes and sickles and to cut down bushes, grass and trees which happened to interfere with a perfect stance.

In short, the quality of the stance is bound to be affected by the general situation, and the player must accommodate himself to that general situation. He may not bend and twist it to suit his convenience.

Therefore, the term "fairly taking his stance" is a relative term, not an absolute one. The player is always limited by the main object of the Rule, which is to avoid improving the position of the ball except as may be done incidentally.

The Rules of Golf Committee had this to say about the knocking down of leaves during a practice swing, in Decision 61-28, issued after a letter on the subject from Mrs. H.F. Wohlers, of San Diego:

Whether a player who knocks leaves down with a practice swing violates the provisions of this Rule is a question of fact and can only be determined by the evidence in each case. In some cases the knocking down of a number of leaves would not help the player and therefore a penalty should not be applied. In other cases, the knocking down of one leaf would help the player and a penalty should be applied.

The words "cut turf" applies to a divot and to newly placed sod. When a divot has been replaced it is considered fixed and its position may not be altered. Assume a ball lies directly in front of a replaced divot which may bother the player as he begins his backswing. It's a violation if he either removes or presses down hard on that divot.

The words "line of play" were put to a severe test in the last round of the 1972 Jackie Gleason tournament when Tom Weiskopf, who was leading, walked about 100 yards from his ball to the 17th green. Tom walked directly *through* a bunker en route to the green. On his way back he meticulously raked the bunker, eradicating his footprints. (It was later established that his footprints were slightly off a direct line between his ball and the hole.) Since his shot to the green was going to be a very lofted pitch, it was obvious that Tom was not trying to improve his line of play by raking the bunker but was instead doing what every courteous golfer should do—rake bunkers. Nevertheless, the incident raised the momentous question of what exactly the "line of play" is and whether Weiskopf, albeit unintentionally, improved his line. Weiskopf was not penalized and won the tournament, but the incident preoccupied the USGA Rules of Golf Committee for months. Eventually it was decided that the line of play "is the direction which the player wishes his ball to take after a stroke plus a reasonable distance on either side of the intended direction and a reasonable distance beyond the intended objective. The line of play is both in the air and on the ground." Weiskopf's path was therefore on his line of play. However, he had not *improved* his line, since all the raking did was restore the bunker to its original condition. The Committee was correct in not penalizing him. (72-32)

As for Rule 17-2, an extreme example of "building a stance" would be to climb on a golf-cart seat to whack away at a ball lodged in a tree. A more common violation occurs when players, faced with taking an uneven stance in a bunker, pound down the side of a bunker with their heels in order to get their feet level.

Some examples illustrating what Rule 17-4 means by "taking any action to influence the position or the movement of a ball" are found in USGA Decisions:

● A player purposely steps on and damages (or improves) his opponent's line of putt. Violation! (58-27)

● A player in a professional event in Wales ingeniously placed his bag parallel to the line of a short putt to shield the line from the wind. Violation! (64-36)

● In the California Amateur Championship at stroke play a competitor who had holed out repaired spike marks on the line of putt of a fellow-competitor. Violation! The player who did the repair job is penalized two strokes. If the player whose line was improved sanctioned the repair job, he too should be penalized two strokes, but under Rule 17-1. If it's found that there was an agreement between the two to repair damage on each other's line of putt, both should be disqualified under Rule 4 for having agreed to waive a Rule. (70-33)

● Player's putt hangs on the lip of the hole in a match. He takes three quick steps forward and then a big jump, landing three feet from the cup. The ball falls into the hole. Jim Rafferty, of Carbondale, Pennsylvania, said that happened on the deciding hole of a friendly match. Violation! (74-10)

RULE 18: LOOSE IMPEDIMENTS
(DEF. 17)

Any loose impediment may be removed without penalty except when both the impediment and the ball lie in or touch a hazard. When a player's ball is in motion, a loose impediment on his line of play shall not be removed.

PENALTY FOR BREACH OF RULE:
Match play—Loss of hole; Stroke play—Two strokes.
(Ball moving after loose impediment touched—Rules 27-1e and 35-1b.)
(Finding ball in hazard—Rule 33-1e.)

A Bad Break
*Because it's in a hazard
this twig may not be
removed. The same applies
to leaves, stones and other
loose impediments*—natural
*objects. On the other hand,
if the twig happened to be a
cigar it could be removed
because a cigar is an
obstruction*—an artificial
*object. (R. 18, Def. 17 and
Def. 20)*

Rule 18 is easy to understand and apply, provided you know that loose impediments, according to Definition 17, are "natural objects not fixed or growing and not adhering to the ball." Sticks, pebbles and stones not solidly embedded, and leaves are all loose impediments.

The prohibition against moving loose impediments in hazards is purposefully severe. Generally speaking, when you've hit your ball into a hazard you've made a mistake, and you have to deal with the problem directly. That means not removing leaves or stones that happen to interfere with a stroke in a bunker. And remember the famous half-eaten-pear decision under Definition 17.

Rule 18 is a positive statement of a golfer's rights. It does not deal with the problem that arises when a ball moves after a loose impediment is touched, but a parenthetical phrase after the Rule directs the reader to the right place—to Rule 27-1e for cases both through the green (one-stroke penalty, and the ball must be replaced) and to 35-1b for cases on putting greens (no penalty, and the ball must be replaced.).

RULE 19: STRIKING AT BALL

RULE 19-1:

BALL TO BE FAIRLY STRUCK AT

The ball shall be fairly struck at with the head of the club and must not be pushed, scraped or spooned.
PENALTY FOR BREACH OF RULE 19-1:
Match play—Loss of hole; Stroke play—Two strokes.

RULE 19-2:

STRIKING BALL TWICE

If a player strike the ball twice when making a stroke, he shall count the stroke and *add a penalty stroke,* making two strokes in all.
(Playing a moving ball—Rule 25.)

Decision 52-101 is the landmark clarification of "fairly struck at." The USGA had been asked to consider a case submitted by O.M. Leland, of Minneapolis, Dean of the University of Minnesota's engineering school, in which there was an obstacle, perhaps a tree trunk, behind a ball so close that when the player addressed the ball, there was only half an inch between the face of the club and the ball. Would the movement of the club to the ball then constitute a stroke? If not, the only recourse was to declare the ball unplayable. The USGA ruled that "such action more than likely would be a push in violation of Rule 19-1" and went on to say:

> *Definition 31 provides that "A stroke is the forward movement of the club made with the intention of fairly striking at and moving the ball." Striking at the ball implies a swing of the clubhead; if there is no such swing, there is no stroke, and any other method of trying to move the ball must be either pushing, scraping or spooning in violation of Rule 19-1. Generally, fairly striking at a ball contemplates only momentary contact between clubhead and ball or whatever intervenes between clubhead and ball.*

I have had problems with Rule 19. During the 1977 Memorial Tournament at Jack Nicklaus' Muirfield Golf Club, I tried to putt my ball out of heavy grass. When I struck the ball it tangled in the grass and I hit it again in a continuation of the same stroke. I immediately —and sorrowfully—called the penalty on myself.

RULE 20: BALL FARTHER FROM THE HOLE PLAYED FIRST

RULE 20-1:

GENERAL

When the balls are in play, the ball farther from the hole shall be played first. If the balls are equidistant from the hole, the option of playing first should be decided by lot.

A player or a competitor incurs no penalty if a ball is moved in measuring to determine which ball is farther from the hole. A ball so moved shall be replaced.

RULE 20-2:

MATCH PLAY

Through the green or in a hazard, if a player play when his opponent should have done so, the opponent may immediately require the player to replay the stroke. In such a case, the player shall drop a ball as near as possible to the spot from which his previous stroke was played, and play in correct order without penalty.

Exception: Three-ball, best-ball and four-ball match play. See Rule 40-1d.

PENALTY FOR BREACH OF RULE 20-2: *Loss of hole.*

(Playing out of turn on putting green—Rule 35-2b.)

> If a competitor play out of turn, no penalty shall be incurred. The ball shall be played as it lies.

The principle is that the ball farther from the hole shall be played first. Here's a summary of what happens when a ball is played out of turn in the three most common forms of play:

Single match: The opponent *may* immediately require the player to replay the stroke. If played through the green or from a hazard, the ball to be replayed is *dropped;* if played on a putting green, the ball *is replaced.* No penalty.

Stroke play: No penalty, and the ball is played as it lies—not played over.

Four-ball match: Through the green or in a hazard there is no penalty and the stroke is not replayed; on the putting green, however, an opponent may require the player who played out of turn to replay the stroke in correct order. No penalty.

RULE 21: PLAYING A WRONG BALL (DEF. 5) OR FROM A WRONG PLACE

> A player must hole out with the ball driven from the teeing ground unless a Rule or Local Rule permit him to substitute another ball.

> a. WRONG BALL
>
> If a player play a stroke with a wrong ball (Def. 5) except in a hazard, *he shall lose the hole.*
>
> If a player play any strokes in a hazard with a wrong ball, there is no penalty provided he then play the correct ball; the strokes so played with a wrong ball do not count in the player's score.
>
> If the wrong ball belong to another player, its owner shall place a ball on the spot from which the wrong ball was played.
>
> When the player and the opponent exchange balls during the play of a hole, the first to play the wrong ball other than from a hazard shall lose the hole; when this cannot be determined, the hole shall be played out with the balls exchanged.
>
> b. BALL PLAYED FROM WRONG PLACE
>
> If a player play a stroke with a ball which has been dropped or placed under an applicable Rule but in a wrong place, *he shall lose the hole.*
>
> **Note:** *For a ball played outside teeing ground, see Rule 13-1.*

a. WRONG BALL

If a competitor play a stroke with a wrong ball (Def. 5) except in a hazard, *he shall add two penalty strokes to his score* and shall then play the correct ball.

If a competitor play any strokes in a hazard with a wrong ball, there is no penalty provided he then play the correct ball.

Strokes played with a wrong ball do not count in a competitor's score.

If the wrong ball belong to another player, its owner shall place a ball on the spot from which the wrong ball was played.

b. RECTIFICATION AFTER HOLING OUT

If a competitor hole out with a wrong ball, he may rectify his mistake by proceeding in accordance with Clause 3a of this Rule, subject to the prescribed penalty, provided he has not made a stroke on the next teeing ground, or, in the case of the last hole of the round, has not left the putting green. *The competitor shall be disqualified* if he does not so rectify his mistake.

c. BALL PLAYED FROM WRONG PLACE

If a competitor play a stroke with a ball which has been dropped or placed under an applicable Rule but in a wrong place, *he shall add two penalty strokes to his score* and play out the hole with that ball. If a serious breach of the applicable Rule is involved, *the competitor shall be disqualified* unless the breach has been rectified as provided by Rule 21-3d.

Note: *For a ball played outside the teeing ground, see Rule 13-2.*

d. RECTIFICATION

If a serious breach of the applicable Rule under Rule 21-3c may be involved and the competitor has not made a stroke on the next teeing ground or, in the case of the last hole of the round, has not left the putting green, the competitor may rectify any such serious breach by *adding two penalty strokes to his score,* dropping or placing a ball in accordance with the applicable Rule and playing out the hole. On completion of the round, the competitor must report the facts immediately to the Committee, which shall determine whether a serious breach of the Rule was involved and, accordingly, whether the score with the ball played under this Rule 21-3d shall count.

Note: *Penalty strokes incurred by playing the ball ruled not to count and strokes subsequently taken with that ball shall be disregarded.*

The first two sections of Rule 21 are straightforward and simple, but the third section, for stroke play, is just plain tricky and onerous. Let's tackle them in order:

General—You may not substitute balls during a hole unless specifically authorized to do so in the Rules. This precludes the use of what some golfers call "putting balls," the nice white round and unscarred ones they would like to use after using a battered veteran off the tee on a water hole.

Match play—As soon as a player plays a wrong ball (except in a hazard) he loses the hole; in four-ball play the errant player is disqualified for that hole but there's no penalty for his partner. As for a ball played from a wrong place, an example of that mistake would be a player's dropping *closer* to the hole after taking relief from ground under repair and then playing a stroke.

Stroke play—When a competitor plays a wrong ball, he immediately suffers a two-stroke penalty and doesn't count any strokes played with the wrong ball. More than that, if the mistake is not *rectified,* the penalty is disqualification. Rectification means returning to play the correct ball *before* teeing off on the next hole, or if the mistake is made on the last hole, before he leaves the putting green.

If a ball is played from the wrong place, the player holes out with that ball and adds two penalty strokes to his score.

Ah, but then we get into the matter of a "serious breach" which contemplates the prospect of a player's gaining an inordinate advantage by the violation. Picture a water hazard 30 yards in diameter right up against a green. The ball enters the hazard in such a way that the player, in taking relief, must drop behind the hazard. But let's assume the player instead drops on the far side of the hazard, next to the green. He hasn't negotiated the hazard. That's a serious breach, and unless it's rectified, the penalty is disqualification.

I've played a wrong ball only once in my professional career. During the 1972 pro tour's Team Championship (four-ball stroke play), my partner was Bob Zender at the Laurel Valley Golf Club, in Ligonier, Pennsylvania. We both pushed our drives to the right on one hole and managed to play each other's balls. We discovered the errors before either of us had played a third stroke. It meant two-stroke penalties for both of us and we had to go back and play correctly. I "birdied" the hole with the correct ball, but our score for the hole was a bogie 5.

Some Rule 21 Decisions to chew on:

● A player swings at a ball, misses and then discovers it wasn't his ball—a query from Indianapolis sports writer Bill Fox.

In match play the player makes a stroke at a wrong ball and loses the hole; in stroke play he incurs a two-stroke penalty. (58-32)

● In stroke play, a player assumed his ball entered a water hazard. As Mrs. Frank Bisbee, of Jacksonville, Florida, told it, the player took relief under Rule 33 by dropping another ball and played it toward the green. The original ball was then found *outside* the water hazard.

The player played a wrong ball. If he searched for the original for less than five minutes, the original ball remains the ball in play and must be played; if the original was found more than five minutes after the search began, the original ball must be considered lost, and the player must proceed under the lost-ball Rule, taking the penalty of stroke and distance in addition to the two-stroke penalty for playing a wrong ball. (60-32)

● A player in stroke play doesn't realize his ball is out of bounds and plays a stroke from OB.

The player played a wrong ball, since the ball was no longer in play once it went out of bounds. He must rectify his error before playing from the next tee or be disqualified. (70-26).

RULE 22: LIFTING, DROPPING AND PLACING

RULE 22-1:

LIFTING

A ball to be lifted under the Rules or Local Rules may be lifted by the player, his partner or another person authorized by the player. In any such case, the player shall be responsible for any breach of the Rules or Local Rules.

Note: *A referee or observer should not lift a ball or mark its position (Defs. 19 and 26).*

RULE 22-2:

DROPPING

a. HOW TO DROP

A ball to be dropped under the Rules or Local Rules shall be dropped by the player himself. He shall face the hole, stand erect, and drop the ball behind him over his shoulder. If a ball be dropped in any other manner and remain the ball in play (Definition 5), *the player shall incur a penalty stroke.*

If the ball touch the player before it strikes the ground, the player shall re-drop without penalty. If the ball touch the player after it strikes the ground, or if it come to rest against the player and move when he then moves, there is no penalty, and the ball shall be played as it lies.

b. WHERE TO DROP

When a ball is to be dropped, it shall be dropped as near as possible to the spot where the ball lay, but not nearer the hole, except when a Rule permits it to be dropped elsewhere or placed. In a hazard, the ball must come to rest in that hazard; if it roll out of the hazard, it must be re-dropped, without penalty.

c. WHEN TO RE-DROP

If a dropped ball roll into a hazard, onto a putting green, out of bounds or more than two club-lengths from the point where it first struck the ground, or come to rest nearer the hole than its original position, it shall be re-dropped, without penalty. If the ball again roll into such a position, it shall be placed where it first struck the ground when re-dropped.

PENALTY FOR BREACH OF RULE 22-2:
Match play—Loss of hole; Stroke play—Two strokes.

RULE 22-3:

PLACING

a. HOW AND WHERE TO PLACE

A ball to be placed under the Rules or Local Rules shall be placed by the player or his partner. A ball to be replaced shall be replaced by the player, his partner or the person who lifted it, on the spot where the ball lay. In any such case,

(continued)

the player shall be responsible for any breach of the Rules or Local Rules.

b. LIE OF BALL TO BE PLACED OR REPLACED ALTERED

If the original lie of a ball to be placed or replaced has been altered, the ball shall be placed in the nearest lie most similar to that which it originally occupied, not more than two club-lengths from the original lie and not nearer the hole.

c. SPOT NOT DETERMINABLE

If it be impossible to determine the spot where the ball is to be placed, through the green or in a hazard, the ball shall be dropped, or on the putting green it shall be placed, as near as possible to the place where it lay but not nearer the hole.

d. BALL MOVING

If a ball when placed fail to remain on the spot on which it was placed, it shall be replaced without penalty. If it still fail to remain on that spot, it shall be placed at the nearest spot not nearer the hole where it can be placed at rest.

PENALTY FOR BREACH OF RULE 22-3:
Match play—Loss of hole; Stroke play—Two strokes.

RULE 22-4:

BALL IN PLAY WHEN DROPPED OR PLACED

A ball dropped or placed under a Rule governing the particular case is in play (Definition 5) and shall not be lifted or re-dropped or replaced except as provided in the Rules.

RULE 22-5:

LIFTING BALL WRONGLY DROPPED OR PLACED

A ball dropped or placed but not played may be lifted without penalty if:—

a. It was dropped or placed under a Rule governing the particular case but not in the right place or otherwise not in accordance with that Rule. The player shall then drop or place the ball in accordance with the governing Rule.

b. It was dropped or placed under a Rule which does not govern the particular case. The player shall then proceed under a Rule which governs the case. However, in match play, if, before the opponent plays his next stroke, the player fail to inform him that the ball has been lifted, *the player shall lose the hole.*

Note: *In stroke play, in the event of a serious breach of Rule 22, see Rules 21-3c and 21-3d.*

Rule 22 requires a good deal of prior knowledge in order that it be used properly. First, the ball should *not be lifted* unless the golfer darn well knows that the Rules authorize him to pick it up. Second, having lifted the ball, he should know *whether the ball should be dropped or placed* when it is put back into play. If it is to be dropped, he should know *where* he may drop it. In some cases the ball is to be dropped as near as possible to the spot from which it was lifted (such as when the ball is embedded in a fairway); in others there's a one-club-length tolerance from the condition (taking relief from ground under repair); and in others there's a two-club-length leeway

How to Drop
Stand erect, face the hole and drop the ball over a shoulder (1). It must be dropped again if it touches the player on the way down, if it rolls nearer the hole, into a hazard, out of bounds, onto a putting green, or more than two club-lengths (2). If the result of the second drop is the same as the first, the ball is then placed on the spot (3) where it struck the ground when it was dropped the second time. (R. 22-2)

Geometry of Ball Dropping

Here's a common drop situation. The ball lies in ground under repair at X. First the player determines the nearest point of relief which, in this illustration, is at Y—just outside the ground under repair area. The player must drop within one club-length of Y but he can't drop in the shaded area of the one club-length circle because that area is either closer to the hole or within ground under repair. That leaves him with the unshaded area. The ball remains in play if it's dropped at Point A even though it rolls outside the circle to point B —which is less than two club-lengths from A. (R. 22 and R. 32-2)

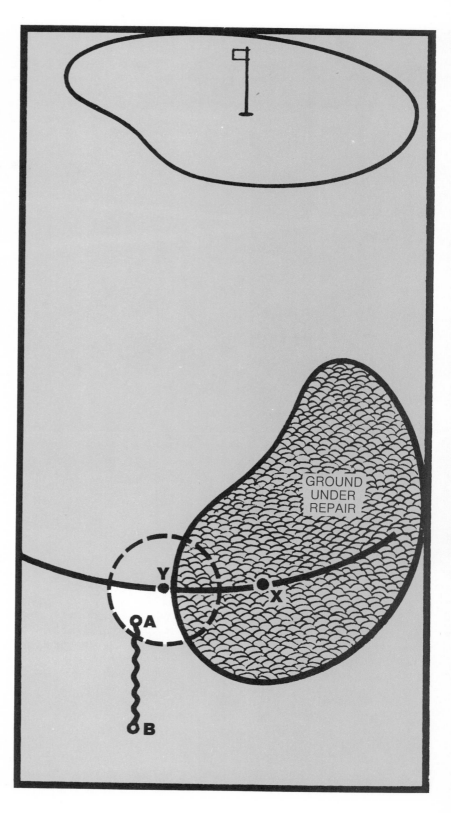

dropping on either side of a lateral water hazard).

Rule 22-2a says there's only one way to drop a ball. Two Decisions of note: According to Decision 54-35, a player may spin the ball when dropping it—indeed, it would be almost impossible to drop a ball so that it does not spin to some degree. Decision 71-16 told Dick Forrester of Houston that a player fulfills the requirement to face the hole when "his feet are pointed approximately in the direction of the hole." He does not violate the Rule by then turning his head.

Drops can result in a player's getting a much more favorable position and at other times a much worse one. This is a break of the game that cannot possibly be equalized by Rules. An example of a bad break would occur when a player lifts his ball in a bunker because his feet are in casual water, but when he drops the ball, it imbeds in sand; a good break would be a player's having a bad lie but taking relief from an obstruction in the rough and having the ball roll into a perfect lie in a fairway.

It often happens that when a player drops a ball, the slope of the ground is such that the ball rolls more than two club-lengths or nearer the hole. Rule 22-2c calls for a three-step procedure:

1. Ball is dropped and it rolls nearer the hole or more than two club-lengths.
2. Ball is dropped again and it again rolls nearer the hole or more than two club-lengths.
3. Ball is then *placed* on the spot where it first touched the ground when it was dropped the second time.

Placing isn't as tricky as dropping, but it can lead to problems. Rule 22-3b deals with what to do when the lie of a ball to be placed has been "altered." Imagine that your ball and your opponent's touch each other in a fairway. He's away, so you mark and lift your ball. When he plays he takes a divot and effectively demolishes your lie. You don't have to place the ball in the hole, nor do you replace the divot and put your ball on it. What you do is place your ball as near as possible to its original position in "the nearest lie most similar to that which it originally occupied, not more than two club-lengths from the original lie; and not nearer the hole."

Jack Nicklaus is superb when it comes to understanding and applying the Rules, but he once cost himself dearly by failing to know Rule 22-4. It happened in the 1973 Masters. His ball had come to rest against a spectator's stool, and the ball moved when the stool was moved. Jack then replaced his ball on a bank which sharply sloped toward the 15th green. There was very little grass to support the ball and Jack was faced with a delicate little pitch. It was not likely he'd get down in two. Ben Crenshaw, with whom Jack was paired, was away, and as Ben prepared to play and then did play, Jack surveyed the green. When he looked back, he saw that his ball had rolled down the slope about fifteen yards to the edge of the green. The ball had actually been at rest for about one minute. Jack's instinctive sportsmanship suggested to him that he had to put the ball back up on the slope. He conferred with an official, and they agreed that the ball had to be replaced. They were wrong! Once the ball was properly placed and remained at rest for a few seconds, it was in play. When it subsequently moved to a new position, it was in play at the new position and should have been played from there. As it happened, Jack took three to get down from the slope and made a par 5. Had he played from the edge of the green, he would have been putting for an eagle 3 and almost surely would not have made worse than a birdie 4. The kicker to this story is that Jack's sportsmanship could also have cost him three penalty strokes under Rule 27: one for picking up his ball when he was not entitled to do so, and two more for failing to replace it on the spot from which it was lifted. There was no penalty, since a player is entitled to assume that an official's ruling is correct. The next morning the official looked Jack up and apologized profusely, but Jack insisted that no apology was necessary, claiming that it was his business to know the Rules.

Rule 22-5 gets the player off the hook if he makes a mistake in dropping or placing, provided he hasn't then made a stroke. Thus, if a player taking relief from a cart path—an obstruction—drops more than one club-length away from the nearest point of relief and learns of the error, he can correct the mistake without penalty.

RULE 23: IDENTIFYING OR CLEANING BALL

The responsibility for playing the proper ball rests with the player. Each player should put an identification mark on his ball.

RULE 23-1:
IDENTIFYING BALL

Except in a hazard, the player may, without penalty, lift his ball in play for the purpose of identification and replace it on the spot from which it was lifted, provided this is done in the presence of his opponent in match play or his marker in stroke play. If the player lift his ball for identification in a hazard, or elsewhere other than in the presence of his opponent or marker, *he shall incur a penalty of one stroke,* and the ball shall be replaced.

(Touching grass, etc. for identification—Rule 17-2.)

RULE 23-2:
CLEANING BALL

A ball may be cleaned when lifted as follows:—From an embedded lie under Rule 16-2; From an unplayable lie under Rule 29-2; For relief from an obstruction under Rule 31; From casual water, ground under repair or otherwise under Rule 32; From a water hazard under Rule 33-2 or 33-3; On the putting green under Rule 35-1d or on a wrong putting green under Rule 35-1j; For identification under Rule 23-1, but the ball may be cleaned only to the extent necessary for identification; or Under a Local Rule permitting cleaning the ball.

If the player clean his ball during the play of a hole except

(continued)

as permitted under this Rule, *he shall incur a penalty of one stroke,* and the ball if lifted shall be replaced.

Note: *If a player who is required to replace a ball fail to do so, the general penalty for breach of Rule 22-3a will apply in addition to any other penalty incurred.*

Before a round I always make a pencil mark in a dimple just to the right of the number on every ball I might use during that round. This relieves me of the nightmare that confronts every golfer at least once in his life when he is sure of the brand, model and number of his ball but then finds a ball of the same brand and number right next to his in the middle of a fairway. Since he can't positively identify either ball as his, what he's got is a lost ball.

Too many golfers mistakenly believe that they are entitled to clean the ball every time the Rules allow it to be lifted. Not so! Rule 23-2 specifies when a ball may be cleaned after it's been lifted. At other times when the ball is lifted, it may not be cleaned. One example would be when a ball is lifted because it interferes with the play of another ball through the green.

Decision 60-27, following a question by Henry Meiers of the Cleveland District Golf Association, dealt with the basic issue of honesty in the game. It's worth remembering:

Q. Is the player the sole judge of identifying his ball? By purposely not identifying his ball, the player could take unfair advantage of certain Rules in some circumstances. Does an opponent or a fellow-competitor have the right to identify the player's ball?

A.: The Rules are written on the assumption that golfers are honest, and there is nothing in the Rules which specifically covers the point.

In equity (Rule 11-4), an opponent or a fellow-competitor has the right to be satisfied about the identification of a ball or the lack of identification, especially as "Each player should put an identification mark on his ball"—see Preamble to Rule 23.

An opponent or a fellow-competitor who suspects that a player has dishonestly not identified his ball should make a claim under Rule 11-1. The referee or the Committee should consider all available information bearing on the matter.

Attention is called to the Committee's authority to impose disqualification under Rules 1 and 36-5.

RULE 24: BALL INTERFERING WITH PLAY

When the player's ball lies through the green or in a hazard, the player may have any other ball lifted if he consider that it interfere with his play. A ball so lifted shall be replaced after the player has played his stroke.

If a ball be accidentally moved in complying with this

(continued)

> Rule, no penalty shall be incurred and the ball shall be replaced.
> *(Lie of ball to be placed or replaced altered—Rule 22-3b.)*
> *(Putting green—Rule 35-2a and 35-3a.)*
> PENALTY FOR BREACH OF RULE:
> *Match play—Loss of hole; Stroke play—Two strokes.*

There's nothing much to worry about in Rule 24. But do understand that the interference can be mental as well as physical. In other words, if it's A's turn to play and B's ball will not interfere with B's stance, stroke or line of play but the position of B's ball distracts or bothers A in some way, A can require B to lift his ball.

And remember that this is one of those instances when the ball may *not* be cleaned after it's lifted.

RULE 25: A MOVING BALL

RULE 25-1:

PLAYING MOVING BALL PROHIBITED

> A player shall not play while his ball is moving.
> *Exceptions:—*
> Ball falling off tee—Rule 14.
> Striking ball twice—Rule 19-2.
> As hereunder—Rule 25-2.
> When the ball only begins to move after the player has begun the stroke or the backward movement of his club for the stroke, he shall incur no penalty under this Rule, but he is not exempted from the provisions for:—
> Ball at Rest Moved by Player, Accidentally—Rule 27-1d.
> Ball at Rest Moving after Loose Impediment Touched—Rule 27-1e.
> Ball at Rest Moving Accidentally after Address—Rule 27-1f.

RULE 25-2:

BALL MOVING IN WATER

> When a ball is in water in a water hazard, the player may, without penalty, make a stroke at it while it is moving, but he must not delay to make his stroke in order to allow the wind or current to better the position of the ball. A ball moving in water in a water hazard may be lifted if the player elect to invoke Rule 33-2 or 33-3.
> PENALTY FOR BREACH OF RULE:
> *Match play—Loss of hole; Stroke play—Two strokes.*

Frankly, I've never been able to figure out why it's necessary to have a Rule prohibiting play while a ball is moving, but I think I understand it now. Suppose your ball is at rest, poised delicately on a slope, and as you approach the ball it begins to roll—toward a water hazard or a boundary. It might be to your advantage to swat at it on the run—but that makes the game into a form of hockey.

The Rules allow for play of a moving ball in water because if a ball is playable in water, it's often difficult to tell whether the ball is moving or not. It seems only right that the player should be allowed a crack at it, moving or not. The most celebrated instance of playing a moving ball in water took place before I was born—during the 1938 U.S. Open at the Cherry Hills Country Club near Denver. Pro Ray Ainsley put his second shot into a creek on the par-4 16th hole and decided the ball was playable. Ainsley made fourteen strokes at the ball in the hazard. Sometimes the ball was moving when he made a stroke and sometimes it wasn't. In any event, he holed out in nineteen—the most strokes ever taken on one hole in our Open.

Golfers are often thrown for a loop by one provision of Rule 25-1. According to Rule 27-1f, if your ball moves once you've addressed it (taken your stance and grounded your club through the green), you are *deemed* to have caused it to move. OK, suppose you lie 2 in the rough, and after you've addressed the ball and begun your stroke, your ball moves. You complete the stroke and hit the ball. Rule 25 says you are not exempted from Rule 27-1f; therefore, you incurred a one-stroke penalty and now lie 4.

RULE 26: BALL IN MOTION STOPPED OR DEFLECTED

RULE 26-1:

GENERAL

a. By Outside Agency

If a ball in motion be accidentally stopped or deflected by any outside agency, it is a rub of the green and the ball shall be played as it lies, without penalty.

b. Lodging in Outside Agency

If a ball lodge in any moving or animate outside agency, the player shall, through the green or in a hazard, drop a ball, or on the putting green place a ball, as near as possible to the spot where the object was when the ball lodged in it, without penalty.

Exception to Rule 26-1: On putting green—Rule 35-1h.

RULE 26-2:

MATCH PLAY

a. By Player

If a player's ball be stopped or deflected by himself, his partner or either of their caddies or equipment, *he shall lose the hole.*

b. By Opponent, Accidentally

If a player's ball be accidentally stopped or deflected by an opponent, his caddie or equipment, no penalty shall be incurred. The player may play the ball as it lies or, before another stroke is played by either side, he may cancel the stroke, place a ball on the spot where the ball previously lay and replay the stroke.

Exception:—Ball striking person attending flagstick—Rule 34-3b.

(continued)

(Ball purposely stopped or deflected by opponent—Rule 17-4.)

(Ball striking opponent's ball—Rule 27-2b.)

RULE 26-3:
STROKE PLAY

a. BY COMPETITOR

If a competitor's ball be stopped or deflected by himself, his partner or either of their caddies or equipment, *the competitor shall incur a penalty of two strokes.* The ball shall be played as it lies, except when it lodges in the competitor's, his partner's or either of their caddies' clothes or equipment, in which case the competitor shall, through the green or in a hazard, drop the ball, or on the putting green place the ball, as near as possible to where the article was when the ball lodged in it.

b. BY FELLOW-COMPETITOR

If a competitor's ball be accidentally stopped or deflected by a fellow-competitor, his caddie, ball or equipment, it is a rub of the green and the ball shall be played as it lies.

Exceptions:—

Ball lodging in fellow-competitor's clothes, etc.—Clause 1b of this Rule.

On the putting green, ball striking fellow-competitor's ball in play—Rule 35-3c.

Ball played from putting green stopped or deflected by fellow-competitor or his caddie—Rule 35-1h.

Ball striking person attending flagstick—Rule 34-3b.

PENALTY FOR BREACH OF RULE:

Match play—Loss of hole; Stroke play—Two strokes.

Note: *If the referee or the Committee determine that a ball has been deliberately stopped or deflected by an outside agency, including a fellow-competitor or his caddie, further procedure should be prescribed in equity under Rule 11-4. On the putting green, Rule 35-1h applies.*

Moving golf balls hit things and people. That's what Rule 26 is about. The player whose ball is stopped by himself, his caddie or a partner is penalized. Were it otherwise, the potential for abuse could include stationing a caddie or partner, like a goalie, in front of bunkers.

Rule 26-2b was changed dramatically in 1980, and the change was welcome and long overdue. From time immemorial, when a player's ball was accidentally stopped or deflected by an opponent, the *opponent* lost the hole. Since such incidents almost always occur because of poor or freakish strokes, the Rule was amended to provide that:

1. There is no penalty in such cases and
2. The player has a choice of either playing the ball as it lies or cancelling the stroke and playing it over.

Thus, there will be no more additions to the tales of horror that have become part of golf's lore under old and despised Rule 26-2b.

Two of my favorites:

*Jim Tom Blair, a first-rate amateur, was about to win the Missouri Amateur Championship. On the decisive hole of the championship, there was no way he could lose—seemingly. Then his opponent's ball slammed into a tree, ricocheted and hit poor Jim Tom, who lost the hole and the match.

*Peter Nissenson of Westchester County in New York was about to take command of his first-round match in the 1976 U.S. Amateur Championship at the Bel-Air Country Club, Los Angeles. Nissenson was sure to get a birdie or par on a par-3 hole while his opponent Charles Lamb was down in a huge concrete culvert that slashes through the second 9 at Bel-Air. Nissenson, knowing full well the perils of old Rule 26-2b, carefully placed both himself and his caddie well behind the culvert. When Lamb made his stroke, the ball didn't get up fast enough. It banged into the concrete embankment in front of him and rebounded straight back. It nicked Nissenson's caddie. Nissenson, who had traveled three thousand miles to suffer this, lost 1 down.

Some Rule 26 Decisions:

● Velma Van Deisen, of Thousand Palms, California, wrote and said that a ball struck a piece of maintenance equipment and was deflected out of bounds. The player claimed she should not be penalized on the grounds that the equipment wasn't supposed to be there.

The ball must be treated as out of bounds. A rather harsh rub of the green is what occurred. (75-8)

● Jack Sargent, of Atlanta, an authority on the Rules, has asked questions that resulted in many Decisions. Here's one:

A player, in stroke play, hits a ball off line; the ball first hits his bag and then his caddie. Is the player penalized four strokes for two violations of Rule 26-3a?

No. Generally, a single penalty is applied to several instances of a breach of a Rule in connection with a single stroke. For example, soling the club by touching the ground or water with it time and again in a hazard entails a single penalty. Ah, but in this case, if the ball had struck his caddie and then went out of bounds, he would have violated two different Rules and paid the consequences for both. (67-1)

RULE 27: BALL AT REST MOVED (DEF. 3)

RULE 27-1:

GENERAL

a. By Outside Agency
If a ball at rest be moved by any outside agency, the player shall incur no penalty and shall replace the ball before playing another stroke.
(Opponent's ball moved by player's ball—Rule 27-2b.)
Note 1: *Neither wind nor water is an outside agency.*
Note 2: *If the ball moved is not immediately recoverable, another ball may be substituted.*
b. During Search
During search for a ball, if it be moved by an opponent, a fellow-competitor or the equipment or caddie of either, no

(continued)

Stop That Outside Agency!

The player is Johnny Bulla; the scene the 1950 U.S. Open Championship at the Merion Golf Club. An outside agency snatched Bulla's ball and made a clean getaway. Whenever an outside agency—be it animal, human or mechanical—moves a ball, the ball is to be replaced without penalty. If the outside agency is a successful thief another ball may be substituted. (R. 27-1a)

penalty shall be incurred. The player shall replace the ball before playing another stroke.

c. By Player, Purposely

When a ball is in play, if a player, his partner or either of their caddies purposely move, touch or lift it, except as provided for in the Rules or Local Rules, *the player shall incur a penalty stroke* and the ball shall be replaced. The player may, however, without penalty, touch the ball with his club in the act of addressing it, provided the ball does not move (Def. 3).

(On putting green—Rule 35-1k.)

d. By Player, Accidentally

When a ball is in play, if a player, his partner, their equipment or either of their caddies accidentally move it, or by touching anything cause it to move, except as provided for in the Rules or Local Rules, *the player shall incur a penalty stroke.* The ball shall be replaced unless the movement of the ball occurs after the player has begun his swing and he does not discontinue his swing.

(Ball accidentally moved when measuring to determine which ball farther from the hole—Rule 20-1.)

(Ball accidentally moved in the process of marking—Rule 35-2a or 35-3a.)

e. Ball Moving after Loose Impediment Touched

Through the green, if the ball move before the player has addressed it but after any loose impediment lying within a club-length of it has been touched by the player, his partner or either of their caddies, the player shall be deemed to have caused the ball to move. *The penalty shall be one stroke.* The ball shall be replaced unless the movement of the ball occurs after the player has begun his swing and he does not discontinue his swing.

(Loose impediment on putting green—Rule 35-1b.)

f. Ball Moving Accidentally after Address

If a ball in play move after the player has addressed it (Def. 1), he shall be deemed to have caused it to move and *shall incur a penalty stroke,* and the ball shall be played as it lies.

RULE 27-2:

MATCH PLAY

a. By Opponent

If a player's ball be touched or moved by an opponent, his caddie or equipment (except as otherwise provided in the Rules), *the opponent shall incur a penalty stroke.* The player shall replace the ball before playing another stroke.

b. Opponent's Ball Moved by Player's Ball

If a player's ball move an opponent's ball, no penalty shall be incurred. The opponent may either play his ball as it lies or, before another stroke is played by either side, he may replace the ball.

If the player's ball stop on the spot formerly occupied by

(continued)

the opponent's ball and the opponent declare his intention to replace the ball, the player shall first play another stroke, after which the opponent shall replace his ball.

(Putting green—Rule 35-2c.)

(Three-Ball, Best-Ball and Four-Ball match play—Rule 40-1c.)

RULE 27-3:
STROKE PLAY

BALL MOVED BY A FELLOW-COMPETITOR

If a competitor's ball be moved by a fellow-competitor, his caddie, ball or equipment, no penalty shall be incurred. The competitor shall replace his ball before playing another stroke.

Exception to penalty:—Ball striking fellow-competitor's ball on putting green—Rule 35-3c.

PENALTY FOR BREACH OF RULE:

*Match play—Loss of hole; *Stroke play—Two strokes (Playing a wrong ball—Rule 21.)*

Note 1: *If a player who is required to replace a ball fail to do so, the general penalty for a breach of this Rule will apply in addition to any other penalty incurred.*

Note 2: *If it be impossible to determine the spot on which a ball is to be placed or if a ball when placed fail to remain on the spot on which it was placed, Rule 22-3 applies.*

*Note 3: *In stroke play, in the event of a serious breach of Rule 27, see Rules 21-3c and 21-3d.*

Rule 26 deals with all the problems that arise when the course of a ball *in motion* is altered. Its partner, Rule 27, takes us through the tangle of possibilities that occur when a ball *at rest* is moved. Let's think about each part of Rule 27:

27-1a—When your ball is moved by a dog or by a golfer playing on another hole, it's been moved by an outside agency and you *must* replace the ball. No penalty. If you can't find your ball and only *think* it may have been moved by an outside agency but aren't sure, all the available testimony and facts must be considered. To proceed under Rule 27-1a, there must be, according to the USGA, "reasonable evidence" to that effect. In the absence of such evidence, the ball must be treated as a lost ball. The player must then proceed under Rule 29-1.

27-1b—There's no penalty if you move your opponent's ball while looking for it. Understand, however, that you are penalized—harsh though it may seem—if you move your own ball while searching for it.

27-1c—Caution: If you so much as reach down and *touch* your ball except as the Rules allow, there is a penalty stroke. The onus is on you to know that the Rules have given you special license whenever you lift your ball.

27-1d—Don't overlook the word "equipment." Definition 7 revealed that a golf cart is part of a player's equipment. When a player runs over his ball while driving a cart, he's violated this Rule. The ball must be *replaced* and a one-stroke penalty is incurred. If the weight of the cart forced the ball down so as to alter the lie, the ball is then *placed,* according to Rule 22-3b, "in the nearest lie most similar to that which it originally occupied, not more than two club-lengths from the original lie and not nearer the hole." The penalty is still one stroke.

There is, however, a catch to this Rule. Suppose the player who moves his ball a couple of feet then plays a stroke without replacing the ball. Not only is he penalized one stroke for having moved his ball, he is also penalized two more strokes for having failed to replace the ball. Total penalty: three strokes.

27-1e—The key word is "deemed." If you move a twig near your ball and the ball then moves, you can argue yourself blue in the face claiming that the movement of the twig didn't cause the ball to move. You are "deemed" to have caused the ball to move.

27-1f—There's that word "deemed" again. Once you've addressed the ball and it moves, that's it—a penalty. When it's windy or when the ball is perched in some precarious position, I take the precaution of not grounding my club and have therefore not addressed it. Remember—Definition 1 tells us that grounding a club is part of addressing a ball through the green.

27-2a—Most violations of the Rules in match play call for loss of hole, but not this one. If your opponent carelessly stumbles and kicks your ball, he incurs a penalty stroke. But be alert: You *must* replace the ball in this instance or else *you lose the hole.*

27-2b—This common situation occurs in match play: Your ball is moved by your opponent's ball. This Rule gives you the choice of replacing the ball or playing it from where it then lies. No penalty. But understand that we're dealing here with a single match, one player against one player. The Rules are different in four-ball match play (two against two). When a player's ball is moved by the ball of an opponent, in a four-ball match, there is no choice—the moved ball must be replaced, as called for in Rule 40-1c.

27-3—There is no penalty when a ball is moved by a fellow-competitor's ball through the green or in a hazard in stroke play. The ball moved *must* be replaced.

Some Rule 27 Decisions:

● A player *accidentally* touches his ball while removing loose impediments but the ball does not move. Harry Easterly, of Richmond, USGA President in 1976–77, asked for a ruling. Result: There is no penalty. Rule 27-1c calls for a penalty only if the ball is *purposely* touched. (76-3).

● Y. Nishihara, of New York City, posed a tough one: A player erroneously thinks he's entitled to relief without penalty from an out-of-bounds stake, drops away and plays out the hole. (A boundary stake, remember, is not an obstruction, according to Definition 20.) The penalty is three strokes: One for lifting his ball when not permitted to do so, and two more for failing to replace it. (64-34)

● Clothier Norman Lapkin, of New York City, wanted to know what happens when a player takes a practice swing in a fairway and accidentally hits his ball off the toe of the club. The player incurs a penalty stroke and the ball *must* be replaced, since he had not made a stroke. A stroke, remember, requires that there be an intention to move the ball. (59-4).

● Kathy Whitworth's ball lay in the rough during the 1970

Women's Open. She took two or three practice swings and the club came in contact with the ground about one foot from the ball. She stepped up to the ball and although she did not ground the club, her club head did touch the grass just behind the ball. The ball then moved half a turn.

The ruling was that it's a question of fact whether the player caused the ball to move. The player was not absolved from a penalty merely because she did not complete addressing her ball by grounding her club. Due to the practice swings and touching the grass, the weight of evidence was against the player in this case. (70-30)

Everyone who has ever played golf has accidentally moved his or her ball. The most common penalty occurs when the player addresses the ball, and the club head touches and moves the ball accidentally. It's happened to me at least half a dozen times.

One of the most famous incidents featuring Rule 27 involved Tom Kite, Jr., in the final round of the Colgate Hall of Fame Classic at Pinehurst in 1978. On the 5th hole of the Pinehurst #2 course Tom was addressing his 2-foot putt for a par 4 when the ball moved only a fraction of an inch. He stepped away and told his marker that he had just incurred a penalty stroke. It turned out to cost him a chance to be in a playoff with me.

RULE 28: BALL UNFIT FOR PLAY

The ball may be deemed unfit for play when it is visibly cut or out of shape or so cracked, pierced or otherwise damaged as to interfere with its true flight or true roll or its normal behavior when struck. The ball shall not be deemed unfit for play solely because mud or other material adhere to it, its surface be scratched or its paint be damaged or discolored.

If a player has reason to believe his ball is unfit for play, the player, after he has announced his intention to proceed under this Rule to his opponent in match play or marker in stroke play, may, without penalty, lift his ball in play for the purpose of determining whether it is unfit. If the ball is so damaged as to be unfit for play, the player may substitute another ball, placing it on the spot where the original ball lay. Substitution may only be made on the hole during the play of which the damage occurred.

If a ball break into pieces as a result of a stroke, a ball shall be placed where the original ball lay and the stroke shall be replayed, without penalty.

A player is not the sole judge as to whether his ball is unfit for play. If the opponent or the marker dispute a claim of unfitness, the referee, if one is present, or the Committee shall settle the matter (Rule 11-2 or 11-3).

PENALTY FOR BREACH OF RULE:
Match play—Loss of hole; Stroke play—Two strokes
(Ball unplayable—Rule 29-2.)

Two 1980 additions, in my opinion, significantly improved Rule 28. The first is a commonsense definition of "unfit for play." Second, it is now clear that an opponent or marker has the right to question a judgment that a ball is unfit for play.

The advent of balls with plastic cores and one-piece balls prompted the Rules-makers to spell out that the stroke is in effect canceled when a ball breaks into pieces.

I'm finicky about the balls I use on the tour. Most of us put a brand-new ball into play on every third hole. Moreover, I won't use a ball on a subsequent hole after I've scarred it playing a bunker shot. I probably average eight balls a round.

RULE 29: BALL LOST (DEF. 6), OUT OF BOUNDS (DEF. 21), OR UNPLAYABLE

RULE 29-1:

LOST OR OUT OF BOUNDS

a. Procedure

If a ball be lost outside a water hazard or be out of bounds, the player shall play his next stroke as nearly as possible at the spot from which the original ball was played or moved by him, *adding a penalty stroke* to his score for the hole. If the original stroke was played from the teeing ground, a ball may be teed anywhere within the teeing ground; if from through the green or a hazard, it shall be dropped; if on the putting green, it shall be placed.

(Ball lost in casual water, ground under repair, etc.—Rule 32-4.)

b. Ascertaining Location

A player has the right at any time of ascertaining whether his opponent's ball is out of bounds.

A person outside the match may point out the location of a ball for which search is being made.

c. Standing Out of Bounds

A player may stand out of bounds to play a ball lying within bounds.

RULE 29-2:

UNPLAYABLE

a. Player Sole Judge

The player is the sole judge as to whether his ball is unplayable. It may be declared unplayable at any place on the course except in a water hazard (Rule 33-2, -3).

b. Procedure

If the player deem his ball to be unplayable, he shall either:—

(i) Play his next stroke as provided in Clause 1a of this Rule *(stroke-and-distance penalty),*

or

(ii) Drop a ball, *under penalty of one stroke,* either (a) within two club-lengths of the point where the ball lay, but

(continued)

Unplayable Lie Options

You have three choices when you declare a ball unplayable through the green: (1) Go back and play from the spot where the previous stroke was played, (2) Drop a ball within two club-lengths of where the ball was declared unplayable, no nearer the hole, as shown by the unshaded area, (3) Imagine a line from the hole to the ball and drop anywhere on an extension of that line. In every case there's a penalty of one stroke. If the ball is unplayable in a bunker, the stroke-and-distance option (1) is still available. Options 2 and 3, however, are modified to the extent that the ball must be dropped within the bunker if either is used. (R. 29-2)

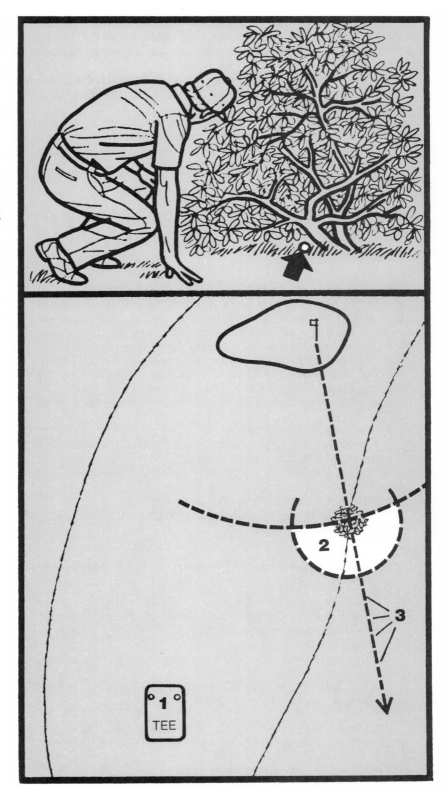

not nearer the hole, or (b) behind the point where the ball lay, keeping that point between himself and the hole, with no limit to how far behind that point the ball may be dropped: if the ball lay in a bunker and the player elect to proceed under this Clause (ii), a ball must be dropped in the bunker.

(Ball in casual water, etc.—Rule 32.)
(Ball unfit for play—Rule 28.)

PENALTY FOR BREACH OF RULE:

*Match play—Loss of hole; *Stroke play—Two strokes.*
***Note:** In stroke play, in the event of a serious breach of Rule 29, see Rules 21-3c and 21-3d.*

Here we have the despised stroke-and-distance penalty, which means that when you knock your tee shot out of bounds (or lose it), your next stroke is played from the tee again and is your *third*—not your second. In other words, you not only lose the distance the ball traveled but have to tack on a penalty stroke as well.

Why? Because otherwise an element of farce would be introduced into the game. Everyone agrees that the concept of allowing for the play of a provisional ball (which we'll talk about next in Rule 30) for a ball that may be lost or out of bounds is sound in that it saves time and trouble. If the penalty were to be distance only (so that the next stroke from the tee after a ball hit out of bounds counted as the second stroke), we would all use the provisional ball not only as a timesaver but as a possible means of getting completely off the hook for playing a bad shot.

Take the par-3 4th hole at the Augusta National Golf Club. It's a hard hole with an impenetrable thicket of cane growth far to the right of the green. If I hit a ball into those canes, I've played an absolutely awful shot. It's not out of bounds and I might have to declare the ball unplayable. There's no way I can make a par and I might well make a 5—or even worse. But suppose Rule 29 were relaxed. Since the ball in the thicket might be lost, I'd be entitled to and would play a provisional ball. Let's say I play this one correctly and knock it eight feet from the hole. I would be tempted not to search for my original ball and instead march right up to the green and have a 50-50 chance of salvaging my par. It would be ludicrous for the Rules to allow situations to develop in which it would sometimes be in the player's best interest to lose his ball.

As a matter of fact, the "distance only" penalty was given a try in 1960 by the USGA in what were labeled "Trial Rules." They were quickly abandoned.

All right, you say, but why does it have to be both stroke *and* distance? If a ball goes out of bounds, why not drop a ball within two club-lengths of the point where the ball crossed the boundary instead of having to go all the way back? Because logic demands that the lost ball and out-of-bounds situations be linked. Wild shots are commonly hit in the direction of boundaries but the ball isn't found. The ball might be out of bounds, but on the other hand, it might just as well be lost in the woods on the course. Since there's no way of knowing for sure where the ball is, the only equitable thing to do is to have the Rules concoct a resolution in which it doesn't matter whether the ball is out of bounds or lost. Either way, back you go to replay the stroke.

The USGA says it gets as much flak on one unusual aspect of Rule 29-2b as on any other Rule. This has to do with what appears to be a general inability to understand that when a ball in a bunker is declared unplayable, the player may avail himself of the stroke-and-distance penalty; the ball may indeed be removed from the bunker and returned to the spot from which the ball was played into the bunker. You can *always* invoke the stroke-and-distance penalty.

Rule 29 Decisions include these:

● Pete Zidnak, of San Jose, California, often submits interesting problems, like this one: A ball is playable in a water hazard, but the player proceeds to knock it out of bounds. When he drops another ball it rolls (less than two club-lengths) into the water; this time he *can't* play it. What to do?

The dropped ball is *in play* and the player's only recourse is to invoke the water hazard Rule (33-2) and drop a ball behind the hazard (taking another penalty stroke in the process). In this case, "the spot at which the ball last crossed the margin of the water hazard" would be the spot where it last crossed *before* it came to rest in the hazard, not the spot where it crossed en route to out of bounds. (72-34)

● A player's ball bounced off a rock, according to E. R. Grilly, of the Los Alamos (New Mexico) Golf Association, and rebounded *behind* him into the woods. He declared it unplayable and elected to drop at the original lie. His opponent protested, claiming that the player was advancing the ball toward the hole without playing a stroke. Who was right?

Answer: The player was entitled to drop at the original lie in the context of the "stroke and distance" penalty, even though, in this rare instance, he gained rather than lost distance. (61-34)

● How do you proceed when a ball is unplayable in a tree? asked Sam Randolph, of Santa Barbara, California.

Answer: You determine the spot directly beneath the ball in the tree and then use Rule 29 just as if the ball were unplayable on the ground at that spot. (63-23)

I still wince when I think what happened to Billy Ziobro during a Hawaiian Open some years ago. I was watching from the window of a hotel adjoining the course. I saw his ball disappear in the foliage of a palm tree. Everyone was sure his ball had lodged in the palm tree, since it was apparent that the ball had entered the tree but hadn't dropped. There was no rough in sight and there were spectators thronging the area. Billy couldn't climb the tree to identify his ball, so had to take the stroke-and-distance penalty for a lost ball instead of declaring the ball unplayable and dropping near the base of the tree for a penalty of one stroke.

RULE 30: PROVISIONAL BALL (DEF. 5)

RULE 30-1:
_____

PROCEDURE

> If a ball may be lost outside a water hazard or may be out of bounds, to save time the player may play another ball
>
> *(continued)*

provisionally as nearly as possible from the spot at which the original ball was played. If the original ball was played from the teeing ground, the provisional ball may be teed anywhere within the teeing ground; if from through the green or a hazard, it shall be dropped; if on the putting green, it shall be placed.

a. The player must inform his opponent or marker that he intends to play a provisional ball, and he must play it before he or his partner goes forward to search for the original ball. If he fail to do so, and play another ball, such ball is not a provisional ball and becomes the ball in play *under penalty of stroke and distance* (Rule 29-1); the original ball is deemed to be lost (Def. 6b).

b. Play of a provisional ball from the teeing ground does not affect the order in which the sides play (Rule 12-2).

c. A provisional ball is never an outside agency.

RULE 30-2:

PLAY OF A PROVISIONAL BALL

a. The player may play a provisional ball until he reaches the place where the original ball is likely to be. If he play any strokes with the provisional ball from a point nearer the hole than that place, the original ball is deemed to be lost (Def. 6c).

b. If the original ball be lost outside a water hazard or be out of bounds, the provisional ball becomes the ball in play, *under penalty of stroke and distance* (Rule 29-1).

c. If the original ball be neither lost outside a water hazard nor out of bounds, the player shall abandon the provisional ball and continue play with the original ball. Should he fail to do so, any further strokes played with the provisional ball shall constitute playing a wrong ball and the provisions of Rule 21 shall apply.

Penalty for breach of Rule:
Match play—Loss of hole; Stroke play—Two strokes.
Note: *If the original ball be unplayable or lie or be lost in a water hazard, the player must proceed under Rule 29-2 or Rule 33-2 or 33-3, whichever is applicable.*

Rule 30 is a welcome timesaver. Although the language of the Rule seems clear enough, Rule 30 is often violated by golfers who seem to think they can play provisional balls whenever the original ball might be in any sort of difficulty.

Here are the pitfalls of Rule 30:

*Beware of getting mixed up with water hazards. Let us assume that a ball is driven toward a water hazard flanked by trees and heavy rough. A provisional ball may be played, since the ball may be lost outside the hazard. But if the original ball is found within the hazard, the provisional ball *must* be abandoned and play is to be continued just as if no provisional ball had been played.

*Moreover, hear this: If a player plays what he erroneously terms a "provisional ball" from the tee only because his original *might* be in a water hazard, he breaks the Rule, since he did not have the right to play a provisional ball.

*When a provisional ball is played because the original may be lost, but the original is found in an unplayable position, the provisional, like it or not, must be abandoned, and play proceeds under Rule 29-2, which has to do with unplayable situations.

*Rule 30 insists that there be an announcement by the player who intends to play a provisional ball. If a ball is driven in the direction of a boundary and the unhappy player says nothing or grunts a sound indicating dissatisfaction and then drives a second ball, that second ball becomes the ball in play, and the original ball, even though it's found on the course, must be abandoned. The player lies 3. The same applies to vague statements such as "I think I better reload" which is not acceptable as an intention to play a provisional ball.

Benjamin Jaques of the New England Golf Association asked the USGA: What's to stop a player from playing a provisional ball on every par-3 hole? Suppose the original is in the woods and the player happens to hole out his provisional ball for a 3. There seems to be nothing in the Rules requiring him to identify his first ball as his, in which case it could be considered a lost ball under Definition 6. Or suppose he plays a provisional ball close to the hole and his original is unplayable up against a tree. Again, what's to stop him from simply continuing play with the provisional? The USGA's answer, in Decision 53-65, is a classic of its kind:

The Rules of Golf are framed on the assumption that golfers play honestly. Permission to play a provisional ball is granted by Rule 30-1 only on the following conditions: first, when a ball may be lost or out of bounds, and, secondly, for the sole purpose of saving time.

If there is no reasonable possibility that the ball may be in either one of the above conditions, the player has no right to play a provisional ball, and if he does so he violates Rule 30-1, penalty for which is loss of hole in match play or two strokes in stroke play. See also Rule 8, which prohibits a practice stroke during the play of a hole, and Rule 37-7, dealing with delay in play.

Dishonestly not identifying a ball may be dealt with by the Committee under Rules 1 and 36-5.

RULE 31: OBSTRUCTIONS (DEF. 20)

RULE 31-1:

MOVABLE OBSTRUCTION
MAY BE REMOVED

Any movable obstruction may be removed. If the ball be moved in so doing, it shall be replaced on the exact spot from which it was moved, without penalty. If it be impossible to determine the spot or to replace the ball, the player shall proceed in accordance with Rule 22-3.

When a ball is in motion, an obstruction on the player's line of play other than an attended flagstick and equipment of the players shall not be removed.

a. INTERFERENCE

Interference by an immovable obstruction occurs when the ball lies in or on the obstruction, or so close to the obstruction that the obstruction interferes with the player's stance or the area of his intended swing. The fact that an immovable obstruction intervenes on the line of play is not, of itself, interference under this Rule.

b. RELIEF

A player may obtain relief from interference by an immovable obstruction, without penalty, as follows:—

(i) *Through the Green:*

Through the green, the point nearest to where the ball lies shall be determined (without crossing over, through or under the obstruction) which (a) is not nearer the hole, (b) avoids interference as defined in Clause 2a of this Rule, and (c) is not in a hazard or on a putting green. He shall lift the ball and drop it within one club-length of the point thus determined on ground which fulfils (a), (b) and (c) above.

Note: *The prohibition against crossing over, through or under the obstruction does not apply to the artificial surfaces and sides of roads and paths or when the ball lies in or on the obstruction.*

(ii) *In a Hazard:*

In a hazard, the player may lift and drop the ball in accordance with Clause (i) above, except that the ball must be dropped in the hazard.

(iii) *On the Putting Green:*

On the putting green, the player may lift and place the ball in the nearest position to where it lay which affords relief from interference, but not nearer the hole.

c. RE-DROPPING

If a dropped ball roll into a position covered by this Rule, or nearer the hole than its original position, it shall be re-dropped without penalty. If it again roll into such a position, it shall be placed where it first struck the ground when re-dropped.

PENALTY FOR BREACH OF RULE:
Match play—Loss of hole; Stroke play—Two strokes.

Golfers tend to pounce on the word "relief" with a sense of reckless joy, ignoring the harsh reality that the relief is limited and precise, and does not offer carte blanche to do anything and everything to avoid inconvenience by artificial objects (obstructions).

First, there are the limitations contained in Definition 20, which says three kinds of artificial objects are *not* obstructions. Therefore, no relief is provided when there is interference by:

a. any object used to define out of bounds, including movable objects such as white stakes;
b. artificial surfaces on the bottom or sides of water hazards;
c. any construction declared by the Committee to be an integral part of the course. The onus is on the Committee to make any

such limitation clear on a scorecard or wherever Local Rules are posted.

The second important limitation in Rule 31 denies relief when an immovable obstruction is on the line of play but is not close enough to interfere with the stance or swing. I'm afraid golfers are misled by what they see on television when "line of sight" relief (dropping to the side of an obstruction on your line) is granted by Local Rule from what are called "temporary immovable obstructions." These include pro-tour necessities such as scoreboards, grandstands and television towers. They are necessarily installed very close to playing areas. There is no such thing as "line of sight" relief in everyday club play.

The third limitation has to do with the maximum relief that is available when a ball lies in or on an obstruction or is so close that it interferes with the stance of swing. Rule 31 offers a procedure for finding "the nearest point" and then allows a drop *within one club-length* of that point. Both the point and the spot at which the ball is dropped can't be nearer the hole than the ball's original resting place, can't be in a hazard or on a putting green, and must be dropped far enough away so as to avoid the very interference for which the relief is granted. See the illustrations and captions accompanying Rule 31 for an exposition of how to drop away from obstructions.

Some other guidelines and cautions in applying Rule 31:

*Whenever the artificial object such as a bench *is movable,* it may be removed. In fact, if relief from a movable obstruction is on the player's mind, it *must* be removed; he does not have the option of lifting and dropping the ball—which might be to his advantage if the ball lies poorly. On the other hand, the relief from movable obstructions is generous in that those on the line of play may be removed. Common movable obstructions on the pro tour include gallery stakes, ropes, TV and telephone wires, and various signs.

*Relief is provided from obstructions in hazards. Movable obstructions (bottles, cigarette butts, etc.) may simply be removed. When the obstruction in a hazard is immovable (a pipe in a water hazard), the ball must always be dropped in the hazard. Gary Player got a big break this way during the 1979 Masters when his ball was playable but down in Rae's Creek near the 13th green. A drainpipe interfered

Movable Obstruction

A bench is something artificial and therefore an obstruction. Obviously I want relief. Since this bench can readily be moved, it's a movable obstruction under the Rules. In that case I do not have the option of dropping away from the bench without penalty. If the ball happened to move when I set the bench aside, I would replace it without penalty. (R. 31-1 and Def. 20)

Immovable Obstruction

I'm entitled to relief because the upright of the shelter interferes with my swing (1). Relief is also provided if the immovable obstruction interferes with my stance (2). But if the immovable obstruction is a problem only because it's on my line, there is no relief (3). I simply play away and —hopefully—hit over or through it (4). (R. 31-2 and Def. 20)

with his swing, and the two-club-length relief available under the 1979 Rules enabled him to drop out of the ditch and up onto a level spot (still in the hazard) where he had a fairly simple chip shot. That was one of the incidents that convinced the USGA that the two-club-length relief under Rule 31 was overly generous.

*One of the most common obstruction situations arises when the stance or swing is interfered with by wires or rope supporting young trees. Understand that the relief applies to the wires or rope but *not to the tree itself,* which means that (a) the "nearest point" must be related to the interfering artificial object and not to the tree, and (b) if the wire or rope doesn't interfere, there is no relief.

*Watch out for sprinkler heads or the plastic caps of irrigation systems located on the aprons of putting greens. The impulse, almost irresistible, is to lift and place the ball off to the side when one of these caps is on your line, especially when your ball is also on the apron and you want to putt it. There is no relief in such a situation just because the darn thing is in your way.

Some Rule 31 Decisions that could come in handy:

● The player's ball is nestled in a hose—a movable obstruction—but he erroneously treats it as an immovable obstruction and drops away instead of moving the hose. William Y. Stembler, of Miami, Florida, asked for help.

Reply: The player lifted a ball when he was not entitled to under the Rules. Under Rule 27-1c he incurs a penalty stroke and has to replace the ball. Failing to do so, he gets hit with two more penalty strokes for a general violation of Rule 27. (53-64) The player should

No Line-of-Sight Relief

My ball is on the apron. I'd prefer to putt, but there's a sprinkler head on my line. The sprinkler head is an immovable obstruction. Since it doesn't interfere with my stance or swing, there's no free relief, so I've got to chip the ball (1). But if the sprinkler head interfered with my stance (2), I'd be entitled to a drop (3). (R. 31-2 and Def. 20)

simply have moved the hose.

● Mitchell Hotra, of Los Angeles, wrote that a player's ball was four or five inches away from a flat sprinkler head which did not interfere with his stance or swing. The player claimed relief, however, on grounds that the covering constituted a mental hazard.

Response: He doesn't get it. Mental interference alone by an obstruction does not entitle the player to relief. (54-19)

● J. Simpson Dean, of Wilmington, Delaware, who had the distinction of winning intercollegiate titles in golf and boxing in the same year, raised a question as to the legality and ethics of using Rule 31 to drop from rough into the fairway. The USGA's reply is memorable:

The object of Rule 31-2 is to relieve the player from interference by an immovable obstruction. As long as this object is attained, the Rule cannot regard any advantage or disadvantage which may incidentally result for the player. This is true generally as well as in the specific case cited because, as has been noted, the Rules of Golf do not distinguish between rough and fairway, both being covered by "through the green" in Definition 35.

This is the technical side and it must also be the ethical side, since the Rule is neutral and could well result in either a good break or a bad break for the player. Since he must accept the bad break when it befalls him, he may also accept a good break. (55-38)

● A player at the Blythefield Country Club in Belmont, Michigan,

asked for relief from a bird's nest, in a plea forwarded by pro John Barnum.

The USGA, in a burst of humanity, tersely said that the nest should be regarded as an immovable obstruction—happily ignoring the reality that a nest is anything but artificial. (58-20)

● An opponent of George Haggarty, of Detroit, found his ball in three feet of water but claimed relief from a bridge which he said interfered with his swing. Given relief, he would be able to drop high and dry within the hazard under Rule 31.

The opponent should *not* be granted relief, since the play of a stroke was a physical impossibility because of the water. "The player may not take purely technical, unrealistic advantage of the Rule." (64-9)

● Mrs. Martin Kaufman of the Bayshore Women's Golf Association in Miami Beach, Florida, said that irrigation control boxes were built near the edges of fairways and asked if it would be proper to install a Local Rule granting "line of flight" relief.

The USGA said no, since the boxes are permanent and therefore not analogous to such things as tents and television equipment, which are given special treatment. (71-6)

● Jack Crist, of Charlotte, North Carolina, then Chairman of the USGA Rules of Golf Committee, thought that the term "nearest point" needed clarification. A Decision was published:

A: When the position of a ball is such that there is interference by

Relief from Cart Paths

An artificially surfaced path is an immovable obstruction. I'm entitled to relief if the ball is on the path (1) or even if the ball isn't on the path but I have to stand on it while addressing the ball (2). To take relief I must stand just off the path and determine where the ball would be if I addressed it with the club I'm going to use for my next stroke (3). That's the nearest point of relief, and I mark it with a tee (4). I can then drop within one club-length of that point (5) not nearer the hole than where the ball was on the path. When you drop (6), be sure the ball doesn't strike your club—a careless violation. (R. 31-2, R. 26-2a, R. 26-3a and Def. 20)

3

4

The Nearest Point

When you take relief from an obstruction, there is only one "nearest point" of relief. The ball can't be moved to whichever side the player prefers. In this situation the nearest point is obviously going to be on the side where I'm standing (1). I mark the nearest point, which is barely off the path (2). Again, the drop may be as much as one club-length away from the nearest point (3). If the ball strikes me on the way down, there's no penalty but it must be dropped again (4). (R. 31-2 and 22-2)

an immovable obstruction as defined in Rule 31-2a or by ground under repair, casual water, etc. as defined in Rule 32-1, there is a specific point (not nearer the hole, nor on a putting green nor in a hazard) nearest to which the ball originally lay on which, if the ball were so positioned, such interference would cease to exist. That point is the "nearest point" within the meaning of the term in Rules 31-2b(i) and 32-2a.

(Exception: If, with respect to immovable obstructions, the ball does not lie in or on an obstruction and an artificially surfaced road or path is not involved, the point in question is the nearest one avoiding interference which can be reached without crossing over, through or under the obstruction.)

After determining the "nearest point," the player shall take relief in accordance with Rule 31-2b(i) or 32-3a.

In determining the "nearest point" on which, if the ball were so positioned, such interference would cease to exist, the club with which the player would expect to play the next stroke would be used. In measuring the club-length from the "nearest point," the player

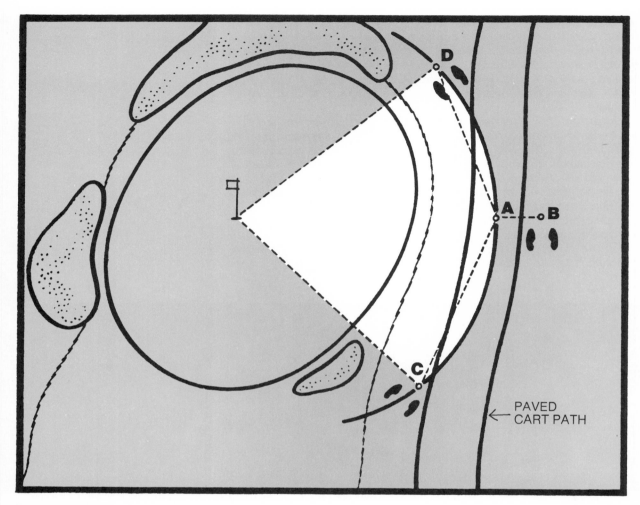

PAVED
CART PATH ←

Dropping from an Obstruction

There are three spots that might qualify as the nearest point of relief whenever there's interference by an immovable obstruction such as a paved cart path. The point that is the shortest distance from the ball (A) must be used. The three possibilities are behind the obstruction (B); on an arc to the left (C); and on an arc to the right (D). Since line A–B is shorter than lines A–C and A–D, the nearest point of relief is B. The same principle applies when relief is taken from ground under repair and casual water. (R. 31-2b and R. 32-3)

would be entitled to use any of the 14 clubs he had selected for the round.

With reference to Rule 31-2b(i), the prohibition against "crossing over, through or under the obstruction" does not apply when measuring from the "nearest point" the one club-length within which the player must drop the ball. (76-33)

RULE 32: CASUAL WATER (DEF. 8), GROUND UNDER REPAIR (DEF. 13), HOLE MADE BY BURROWING ANIMAL

RULE 32-1:

INTERFERENCE

Interference by casual water, ground under repair, or a hole, cast or runway made by a burrowing animal, a reptile or a bird occurs when a ball lies in or touches any of these conditions or when the condition interferes with the player's stance or the area of his intended swing. If interference exists, the player may either play the ball as it lies or take relief as provided in Clause 3 of this Rule.

RULE 32-2:

FINDING BALL

If a ball lying in casual water, ground under repair or a hole, cast or runway made by a burrowing animal, a reptile or a bird is not visible, the player may probe for it. If the ball be moved in such search, no penalty shall be incurred, and the ball shall be replaced unless the player elect to proceed under Clause 3 of this Rule.

RULE 32-3:

RELIEF

If the player elect to take relief, he shall proceed as follows:—

a. *Through the Green*—Through the green, the point nearest to where the ball lies shall be determined which (a) is not nearer the hole, (b) avoids interference by the condition, and (c) is not in a hazard or on a putting green. The player shall lift the ball and drop it without penalty within one club-length of the point thus determined on ground which fulfils (a), (b) and (c) above.

b. *In a Hazard*—In a hazard, the player shall lift and drop the ball either:—

Without penalty, in the hazard as near as possible to the spot where the ball lay, but not nearer the hole, on ground which affords maximum relief from the condition;

or,

Under penalty of one stroke, outside the hazard, but not nearer the hole, keeping the spot where the ball lay between himself and the hole.

c. *On the Putting Green*—On the putting green, or if such

(continued)

111

Casual Water

The ball lies in casual water (1), so I'm entitled to take relief by first determining the nearest point that both avoids the casual water and is not nearer the hole (2). I'm entitled to clean the ball (3). The drop is limited to one club-length from the nearest point (4). If the ball should roll back into casual water or into a position so that the casual water interferes with my stance after the drop, I must drop again (5). If I have to stand in casual water, I'm also entitled to relief even though the ball sits high and dry (6). The nearest point would be where the ball would lie when I've taken a stance outside but as close as possible to the casual water (7). (R. 32 and Def. 8)

3

4

5

6

7

Ground Under Repair

The relief procedure for ground under repair and casual water are the same. I can take relief if the ball is in ground under repair (1) or if I have to stand in the area (2). Relief, of course, is optional. If I like the lie, I'll simply play the ball without taking relief. (R. 32 and Def. 8)

condition on the putting green intervene between a ball lying on the putting green and the hole, the player shall lift the ball and place it without penalty in the nearest position to where it lay which affords maximum relief from the condition, but not nearer the hole nor in a hazard.

RULE 32-4:
BALL LOST

a. *Outside a Hazard*—If a ball be lost under a condition covered by this Rule, except in a hazard, the player may take relief as follows: the point nearest to where the ball last crossed the margin of the area shall be determined which (a) is not nearer the hole than where the ball last crossed that margin, (b) avoids interference by the condition, and (c) is not in a hazard or on a putting green. He shall drop a ball without penalty within one club-length of the point thus determined on ground which fulfils (a), (b) and (c) above.

b. *In a Hazard*—If a ball be lost in a hazard under a condition covered by this Rule, the player may drop a ball either:—

Without penalty, in the hazard, but not nearer the hole than the spot at which the ball last crossed the margin of the area, on ground which affords maximum relief from the condition;

or,

Under penalty of one stroke, outside the hazard, but not nearer the hole, keeping the spot at which the ball last crossed the margin of the hazard between himself and the hole.

In order that a ball may be treated as lost under a condition covered by this Rule, there must be reasonable evidence to that effect.

RULE 32-5:
RE-DROPPING

If a dropped ball roll into the area from which relief was taken, or come to rest in such a position that that area still affects the player's stance or the area of his intended swing, the ball shall be re-dropped, without penalty. If the ball again roll into such a position, it shall be placed where it first struck the ground when re-dropped.

PENALTY FOR BREACH OF RULE:
Match play—Loss of hole; Stroke play—Two strokes.

The word "interference" doesn't always click as it should with readers of the Rules of Golf. "Gets in the way of" or "intervenes" are helpful dictionary definitions. In any event, you are entitled to relief under Rule 32 not only because your ball lies in ground under repair but also if you have to stand in it, even though the ball lies outside the area. The same applies to casual water and burrowing-animal holes.

Speaking of burrowing-animal holes, the USGA said the final words on the subject in Decision 72-17 in reply to a question by Don Siok, the pro at the Atlantic City (New Jersey) Country Club, asking whether relief should be granted from holes made by a dog who digs and leaves behind heaps of earth.

> *A burrow is a hole or tunnel in the ground made by certain animals, such as rabbits, moles, ground hogs and prairie dogs for shelter and habitation. Thus, a "burrowing animal" is an animal that makes a hole in which it may live. A hole made by a dog is not a burrowing animal hole since dogs do not dig holes for habitation or shelter. There is no free relief under the Rules from holes made by dogs or other non-burrowing animals unless such areas are defined as ground under repair by the Committee under Definition 13.*

The extent of relief after determining the nearest point was reduced to one club-length in 1980. The same is true of relief from obstructions under Rule 31. The two-club-length drop was just too generous in that it often completely changed the nature of a shot instead of providing fair relief. So now the Rules talk of a drop of *one* club-length after determining the nearest point for obstructions, ground under repair, casual water and holes, casts or runways made by burrowing animals, reptiles and birds, and a wrong putting green.

The *two*-club-length drop continues to apply for one of three options when a ball is declared unplayable and when a ball is dropped on either side of a lateral water hazard. See the diagram describing the lateral water hazard options.

Determining "the nearest point" is the hardest part of applying Rule 32. It might help to think that there are three possible points to consider every time but only one of the three is *the nearest point* in the sense that your ball will have traveled the shortest distance to reach that point. Once you find that point, then you get the additional one-club-length leeway.

Note that on the putting green the relief is liberal in that it allows you to lift, move and *place* the ball to avoid intervention by casual water. However, if the ball is not on the putting green, you get to complain, but that's all. Thus, if your ball is just off the green, not interfered with by casual water, but there is a puddle on your line, you get no relief.

Remember that there is no such thing, by Definition 8, as casual water in a water hazard—but there may be casual water in a bunker.

Rule 32 Decisions include 64-5, which deals with a number of ground under repair situations:

● A player has a bad lie in ground under repair and wants to drop *within* the ground under repair.

He can't do it; he must drop on ground which avoids the condition, i.e., outside the ground under repair.

● A player drops outside ground under repair as per Rule 32-3a, but the ball rolls back into ground under repair. It has rolled less than one club-length and no nearer the hole. He likes the lie. May he play?

No. He must re-drop.

● A player drops outside ground under repair, but now his stance is in the ground under repair. Must he drop again?

Yes.

● What can a golfer do when a bunker is completely covered by casual water? Warren Orlick, of Orchard Lake, Michigan, a former PGA President, wanted to know.

He may drop it in the bunker in the shallowest casual water as near as possible to the spot where the ball first lay, but not nearer the hole. (55-36)

● Jim Summers, pro at the Alta Sierra Country Club, Grass Valley, California, was asked to handle this situation: A player's ball lay in the narrow crevice of a tree. A stroke at the ball was a physical impossibility, but when the player took his stance, one of his feet was on a burrowing-animal hole. Was he entitled to invoke Rule 32?

No. "A player should be deprived of the right to take purely technical, unrealistic advantage of Rule 32-2a." (70-42)

RULE 33: HAZARDS (DEF. 14)

RULE 33-1:

TOUCHING HAZARD PROHIBITED

When a ball lies in or touches a hazard or a water hazard, nothing shall be done which may in any way improve its lie. Before making a stroke, the player shall not touch the ground in the hazard or water in the water hazard with a club or otherwise, nor touch or move a loose impediment lying in or touching the hazard, nor test the condition of the hazard or of any similar hazard; subject to the following considerations:—

a. STANCE

The player may place his feet firmly in taking his stance.

b. TOUCHING FIXED OR GROWING OBJECT

In addressing the ball or in the stroke or in the backward movement for the stroke, the club may touch any wooden or stone wall, paling or similar fixed object or any grass, bush, tree, or other growing substance (but the club may not be soled in the hazard).

c. OBSTRUCTIONS

The player is entitled to relief from obstructions under the provisions of Rule 31.

d. LOOSE IMPEDIMENT OUTSIDE HAZARD

Any loose impediment not in or touching the hazard may be removed.

e. FINDING BALL

If the ball be covered by sand, fallen leaves or the like, the player may remove as much thereof as will enable him to see the top of the ball. If the ball be moved in such removal, no penalty shall be incurred, and the ball shall be replaced.

If the ball is believed to be lying in water in a water hazard, the player may probe for it with a club or otherwise. If the ball be moved in such search, no penalty shall be incurred; the ball shall be replaced, unless the player elect to proceed under Clause 2 or 3 of this Rule.

The ball may not be lifted for identification.

f. PLACING CLUBS IN HAZARD

The player may, without penalty, place his clubs in the hazard prior to making a stroke, provided nothing is done which may improve the lie of the ball or constitute testing

(continued)

Touching a Hazard
Before you play a stroke in a hazard the ground (or water in a water hazard) must not be touched. When a ball lies in a hazard it is addressed as soon as the player takes a stance (1). If the club touches the sand during the backswing, there's a violation (2). (R. 33-1 and Def. 1)

Touching Grass in a Hazard
When a ball is playable in a water hazard it's often surrounded by tall grass (1). In the act of addressing the ball I'm permitted to touch the grass (2), but it would be a violation to ground the club (3). (R. 33-1b)

Obstructions in Hazards

It's okay to remove obstructions—artificial things—from hazards (1). When it seems likely that removing an obstruction will cause the ball to move, I'll first mark the position of the ball with a coin so that I can be precise in replacing it (2 and 3). (R. 33-1c, R. 31-1, Def. 20)

Buried in Sand

When a ball is completely covered by sand (1), all I'm entitled to do is brush aside enough sand that I can see the top of a ball (2)—but no more. It doesn't matter if I can't identify the ball, since there's no penalty for playing a wrong ball in a hazard. (R. 33-1e, R. 21-2a, R. 21-3a)

the soil.

g. SMOOTHING IRREGULARITIES

There is no penalty should soil or sand in the hazard be smoothed by the player after playing a stroke, or by his caddie at any time without the authority of the player, provided nothing is done that improves the lie of the ball or assists the player in his subsequent play of the hole.

h. CASUAL WATER, GROUND UNDER REPAIR

The player is entitled to relief from casual water, ground under repair, and otherwise as provided for in Rule 32.

i. INTERFERENCE BY A BALL

The player is entitled to relief from interference by another ball under the provisions of Rule 24.

A Time-Saver

The Rules permit you to place clubs or a rake in hazard while playing a stroke. Carrying more than one club or a rake into hazards can often save time. (R. 33-1f)

If a ball lie or be lost in a water hazard (whether the ball lie in water or not), the player may drop a ball *under penalty of one stroke,* either:—

a. Behind the water hazard, keeping the spot at which the ball last crossed the margin of the water hazard between himself and the hole, and with no limit to how far behind the water hazard the ball may be dropped,

or

b. As near as possible to the spot from which the original ball was played; if the stroke was played from the teeing ground, the ball may be teed anywhere within the teeing ground.

Note: *If a ball has been played from within a water hazard and has not crossed any margin of the hazard, the player may drop a ball behind the hazard under Rule 33-2a.*

If a ball lie or be lost in a lateral water hazard, the player may, *under penalty of one stroke,* either:—

a. Play his next stroke in accordance with Clause 2a or 2b of this Rule,

or

b. Drop a ball outside the hazard within two club-lengths of (i) the point where the ball last crossed the margin of the hazard or (ii) a point on the opposite margin of the hazard equidistant from the hole. The ball must be dropped and come to rest not nearer the hole than the point where the original ball last crossed the margin of the hazard.

Note: *If a ball has been played from within a lateral water hazard and has not crossed any margin of the hazard, the player may drop a ball outside the hazard under Rule 33-3b.*

Penalty for breach of Rule:

*Match play—Loss of hole; *Stroke play—Two strokes.*

***Note:** In stroke play, in the event of a serious breach of Rule 33, see Rules 21-3c and 21-3d.*

Note 2: *It is a question of fact whether a ball lost after having been struck toward a water hazard is lost inside or outside the hazard. In order to treat the ball as lost in the hazard, there must be reasonable evidence that the ball lodged therein. In the absence of such evidence, the ball must be treated as a lost ball and Rule 29-1 applies.*

I've always been puzzled by the seeming contradiction in the Rules prohibiting me to test the condition of a hazard in Rule 33-1 but allowing me to take a firm stance in Rule 33-1a. The USGA, in Decision 55-49, wrestled with this contradiction by saying: "Obviously, there is a gray area between the two clauses. The gray area is a necessary evil inasmuch as it would be unfair to prohibit a player from taking a firm stance when his ball lay in the sand. Whether a player infringes on this gray area to his own advantage is often a matter which can be controlled only by his own conscience."

Some keys to the use of Rule 33:

Water-Hazard Options

You can do one of three things when your ball comes to rest in a water hazard: (1) Assuming the ball is playable, go right ahead and play it without penalty. (2) Imagine a line that runs from the hole to the point where the ball crossed the margin of the hazard. You can drop on an extension of that line for a penalty of one stroke. (3) Use the stroke-and-distance option. In this illustration, that would mean returning to the tee where the next stroke would be your third. Note that you cannot drop along the line of the ball's flight. (R. 33-2)

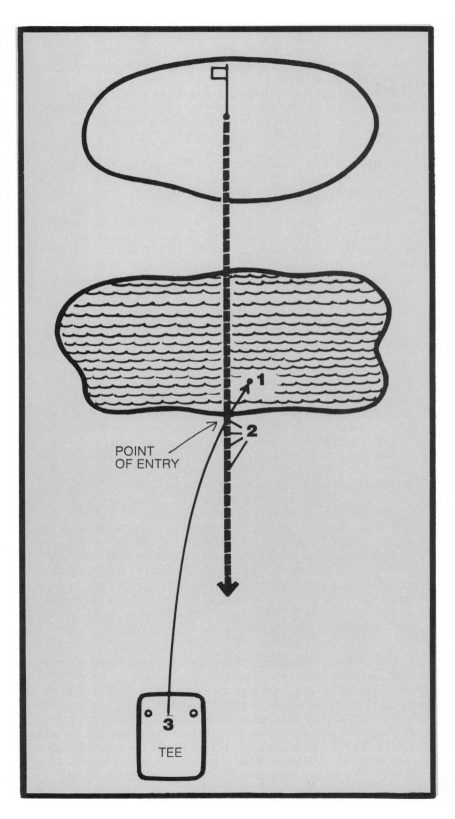

POINT
OF ENTRY

TEE

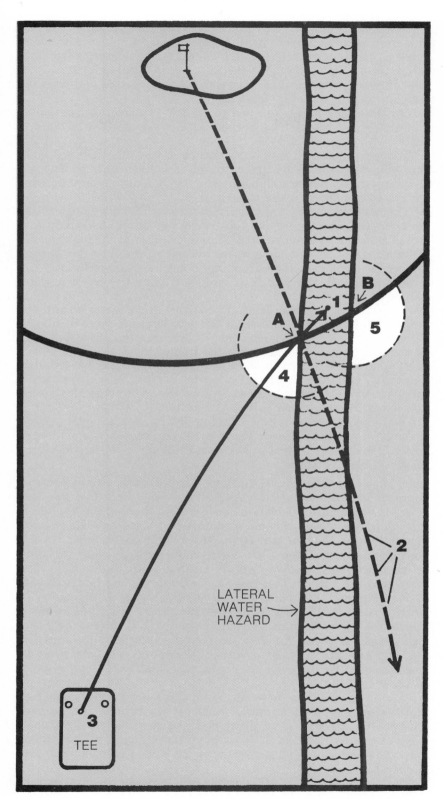

Lateral Water-Hazard Options

There are five options when a ball is within a lateral water hazard. Three are the same as those for a water hazard: (1) Play the ball as it lies without penalty. (2) Drop behind the hazard on a line formed by the hole and the point (A) where the ball entered the hazard with a penalty stroke added. (3) Use the stroke-and-distance option. The other two options also call for a penalty stroke. You may drop within two club-lengths of A no nearer the hole (4) or on the opposite side of the hazard (5). The reference point on the opposite side is B, which is the same distance from the hole as A. (R. 33-3)

LATERAL WATER HAZARD

TEE

*Remember that you may not move loose impediments in a hazard, and that loose impediments include stones and leaves. If you so much as brush one with your club during your backswing (which is before the stroke), you violate the Rule. Accidentally kicking a loose impediment, provided it is not related to the stroke and does not improve the lie, is not a violation.

*On the other hand, you are permitted to move obstructions—man-made objects, such as bottles, candy wrappers and cigarette butts.

*There's a common misconception that you can't change clubs once you've entered a hazard with one in hand. Not true. You can also carry more than one club into a hazard, make your selection and set the others down in the hazard.

*There's no penalty for playing a wrong ball from within any hazard, but at the same time, you are not permitted to identify your ball in a hazard. All you're entitled to is the sight of the top of *a* ball.

*When dropping outside a water hazard or lateral water hazard, the options do not include dropping along the "line of flight."

*Fundamental, but worth affirming: If your ball is in a water hazard and can't be found, is unplayable, or you opt not to play it, the penalty is one stroke. Thus, if you drive into a water hazard and drop a ball behind the hazard, your next stroke is your third.

*Soling the club in a hazard means touching the ground or sand or water in a water hazard with the sole of the club.

*If your ball is buried by sand in a bunker, you may use a club or a rake to find it, but if the ball is moved, it must be replaced, which means that it should be covered by enough sand so that all that can be seen is the top of the ball.

*You may not treat a ball as being lost in a hazard just because it might be in the hazard. There must be "reasonable evidence," which the USGA clarified in Decision 61-31 for J. Walter McGarry, of Vero Beach, Florida.

A: The term "reasonable evidence" is purposely and necessarily broad so as to permit sensible judgments to be reached on the basis of all the relevant circumstances of particular cases. As applied in this context, a player may not deem his ball lost in a water hazard simply because the ball may be in the hazard. The evidence must be preponderantly in favor of its being in the hazard or the ball must be considered lost and the player must proceed under Rule 29-1. Physical conditions in the area, of course, have a great deal to do with it. For example, if a water hazard is surrounded by a fairway on which a ball could hardly be lost, the existence of reasonable evidence that the ball is in the hazard would be more likely than if there were deep rough all about. Referring to the particular case you mention, it is quite true that a splash would not necessarily provide the reasonable evidence. We all know that splashing balls sometimes skip out of hazards.

I've said earlier that there is a consensus among golfers who care that the game is a better game if we all play by the same Rules, even if we don't agree with all of them. For me that principle is put to its sternest test by Decision 64-18, which I don't like at all but expose to readers of this book with the vow to grin and bear it should it ever happen to me.

What 64-18 says is this: If your ball enters a water hazard and the

Flagstick Attended

When a green is elevated, it isn't always possible to see the flagstick in the hole when you address the ball. In that case the flagstick may be held up even as the stroke is being played.
(R. 34-1)

Striking the Flagstick

When I putt from off the green I may prefer to have the flagstick remain in the hole, since there's no penalty for striking the flagstick from off the green (1). But when the ball is played from on the green, there is a penalty for striking the flagstick, which should either be attended (2) or set aside. (R. 34-3)

flow of water carries it out of bounds, the player is not entitled to relief under Rule 33-2. Instead, the ball lies out of bounds.

RULE 34: THE FLAGSTICK (DEF. 12)

Before and during the stroke, the player may have the flagstick attended, removed or held up to indicate the position of the hole. This may be done only on the authority of the player before he plays his stroke. If the flagstick be attended or removed by an opponent, a fellow-competitor or the caddie of either with the knowledge of the player and no objection is made, the player shall be deemed to have authorized it.

If a player or a caddie attend or remove the flagstick or stand near the hole while a stroke is being played, he shall be deemed to attend the flagstick until the ball comes to rest.

If the flagstick be not attended before the stroke is played, it shall not be attended or removed while the ball is in motion.

a. Match Play

In match play, an opponent or his caddie shall not attend or remove the flagstick without the knowledge or authority of the player.

b. Stroke Play

In stroke play, if a fellow-competitor or his caddie attend or remove the flagstick without the knowledge or authority of the competitor, and if the ball strike the flagstick or the person attending it, it is a rub of the green, there is no penalty, and the ball shall be played as it lies.

Penalty for breach of Rule 34-1 and -2:
Match play—Loss of hole; Stroke play—Two strokes.

The player's ball shall not strike either:—

a. The flagstick when attended or removed by the player, his partner or either of their caddies, or by another person with the knowledge or authority of the player; or

b. The player's caddie, his partner or his partner's caddie when attending the flagstick, or another person attending the flagstick with the knowledge or authority of the player, or equipment carried by any such person; or

c. The flagstick in the hole, unattended, when the ball has been played from the putting green.

Penalty for breach of Rule 34-3:
Match play—Loss of hole; Stroke play—Two strokes, and the ball shall be played as it lies.

Wedged Against the Flagstick

A ball is not in the hole until all of it is below the level of the hole. When the ball is jammed against the flagstick (1) and some of it is higher than the hole, the flagstick should be carefully removed (2) so that the ball falls into the hole (3). If you're not careful and the ball pops out of the hole, it is to be placed on the lip of the hole without penalty. (R. 34-4 and Def. 4)

1

2

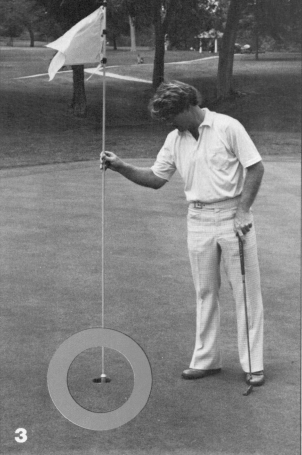

3

If the ball rest against the flagstick when it is in the hole, the player shall be entitled to have the flagstick removed, and if the ball fall into the hole the player shall be deemed to have holed out at his last stroke; otherwise, the ball, if moved, shall be placed on the lip of the hole, without penalty.

The flagstick exists in order to indicate the location of the hole. Its use incidentally as a backstop has been a subject of controversy and the cause of many Rules changes over the years, but the Rule is now happily settled into a form we all understand:

*If your ball is *on* the putting green and it strikes the flagstick, whether it's attended or unattended, it is a loss of hole in match play and two strokes in stroke play.

*If your ball is *off* the green, you may use the flagstick as a backstop—there is no penalty for striking it as long as it is not attended.

RULE 35: THE PUTTING GREEN (DEF. 25)

a. TOUCHING LINE OF PUTT

The line of the putt must not be touched except as provided in Clauses 1b, 1c and 1d of this Rule, or in measuring (Rule 20-1), or in removing movable obstructions (Rule 31-1), but the player may place the club in front of the ball in addressing it without pressing anything down.

b. LOOSE IMPEDIMENTS

The player may move sand, loose soil or any loose impediments on the putting green by picking them up or brushing them aside with his hand or a club without pressing anything down. If the ball be moved, it shall be replaced, without penalty.

c. REPAIR OF HOLE PLUGS AND BALL MARKS

The player or his partner may repair an old hole plug or damage to the putting green caused by the impact of a ball. If the player's ball lie on the putting green, it may be lifted to permit repair and shall be replaced on the spot from which it was lifted; in match play the ball must be replaced immediately if the opponent so requests.

If a ball be moved during such repair, it shall be replaced, without penalty.

d. LIFTING AND CLEANING BALL

A ball lying on the putting green may be lifted, without penalty, cleaned if desired, and replaced on the spot from which it was lifted; in match play the ball must be replaced immediately if the opponent so requests.

e. DIRECTION FOR PUTTING

When the player's ball is on the putting green, the player's

(continued)

Don't Repair Spike Marks

The line of putt is sacrosanct. It is not to be improved unless the Rules specify exceptions—e.g., repairing ball marks, removing loose impediments. This most definitely means that irregularities on the line of putt, such as raised tufts of grass, may not be tamped down, as is being done here. (R. 35-1)

caddie, his partner or his partner's caddie may, before the stroke is played, point out a line for putting, but the line of the putt shall not be touched in front of, to the side of, or behind the hole.

While making the stroke, the player shall not allow his caddie, his partner or his partner's caddie to position himself on or close to an extension of the line of putt behind the ball.

No mark shall be placed anywhere on the putting green to indicate a line for putting.

f. TESTING SURFACE

During the play of a hole, a player shall not test the surface of the putting green by rolling a ball or roughening or scraping the surface.

g. OTHER BALL TO BE AT REST

While the player's ball is in motion after a stroke on the putting green, an opponent's or a fellow-competitor's ball shall not be played or touched.

h. BALL IN MOTION STOPPED OR DEFLECTED

If a ball in motion after a stroke on the putting green be stopped or deflected by, or lodge in, any moving or animate outside agency, the stroke shall be cancelled and the ball shall be replaced.

Note: *If the referee or the Committee determine that a ball has been deliberately stopped or deflected by an outside agency, including a fellow-competitor or his caddie, further procedure should be prescribed in equity under Rule 11-4.*

i. BALL OVERHANGING HOLE

When any part of the ball overhangs the edge of the hole, the owner of the ball is not allowed more than a few seconds to determine whether it is at rest. If by then the ball has not fallen into the hole, it is deemed to be at rest.

(continued)

j. BALL ON A WRONG PUTTING GREEN

If a ball lie on a putting green other than that of the hole being played, the point nearest to where the ball lies shall be determined which (a) is not nearer the hole and (b) is not in a hazard or on a putting green. The player shall lift the ball and drop it without penalty within one club-length of the point thus determined on ground which fulfils (a) and (b) above.

Note: *Unless otherwise stipulated by the Committee, the term "a putting green other than that of the hole being played" includes a practice putting or pitching green lying within the boundaries of the course.*

k. BALL TO BE MARKED WHEN LIFTED

Before a ball on the putting green is lifted, its position shall be marked. If the player fail so to mark the position of the ball, *the player shall incur a penalty of one stroke* and the ball shall be replaced.

(Lifting and placing—Rule 22.)

Note: *The position of a lifted ball should be marked by placing a ball-marker or other small object on the putting green, immediately behind the ball. If the marker interfere*

(continued)

**Don't Use a Hat
As a Brush**
You are allowed to pick up or brush aside loose impediments on the line of putt. But all you can use are your hands or a club. If anything else is used—a hat, for instance—it's a violation. (R. 35-1b)

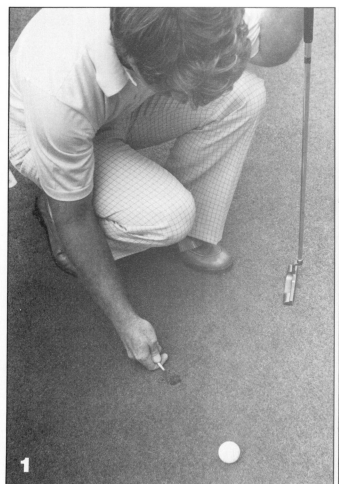

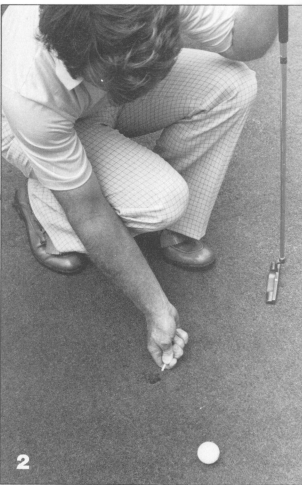

with the play, stance or stroke of another player, it should be placed one or more putterhead-lengths to one side.

1. STANDING ASTRIDE OR ON LINE OF PUTT PROHIBITED

The player shall not make a stroke on the putting green from a stance astride, or with either foot touching, the line of the putt or an extension of that line behind the ball. For the purpose of Rule 35-1L only, the line of putt does not extend beyond the hole.

PENALTY FOR BREACH OF RULE 35-1:
Match play—Loss of hole; Stroke play—Two strokes.

RULE 35-2:

MATCH PLAY

a. BALL INTERFERING WITH PLAY

When the player's ball lies on the putting green, if the player consider that the opponent's ball interfere with his

(continued)

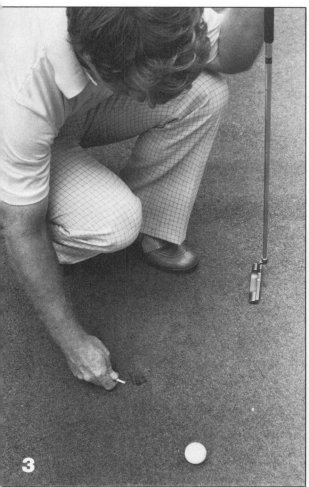

Repairing Ball Marks

Ball marks on putting greens may be repaired (1). As a matter of fact, they should be repaired. I use a tee to loosen the soil around the mark (2). After the compacted soil has been loosened at several positions, I pull the turf toward the center of the ball mark (3). The smoothing process can be done in any reasonable manner. I use my putter (4). (R. 35-1c and Etiquette)

play, he may require that the opponent's ball be lifted. The opponent's ball shall be replaced after the player has played his stroke. If the player's ball stop on the spot formerly occupied by the lifted ball, the player shall first play another stroke before the lifted ball is replaced.

If a ball be accidentally moved in complying with this Rule, no penalty shall be incurred and the ball shall be replaced.

b. PLAYING OUT OF TURN

If a player play when his opponent should have done so, the opponent may immediately require the player to replay the stroke, in which case the player shall replace his ball and play in correct order, without penalty.

c. OPPONENT'S BALL DISPLACED

If the player's ball knock the opponent's ball into the hole, the opponent shall be deemed to have holed out at his last

(continued)

Direction for Putting

My caddie or my partner can use the flagstick to indicate the line of putt, but if he so much as touches the line with the flagstick I would be penalized. (R. 35-1e)

stroke.

If the player's ball move the opponent's ball, the opponent may replace it, but this must be done before another stroke is played by either side. If the player's ball stop on the spot formerly occupied by the opponent's ball, and the opponent declare his intention to replace his ball, the player shall first play another stroke, after which the opponent shall replace his ball.

(Three-Ball, Best-Ball and Four-Ball match play—Rule 40-1c.) *(continued)*

No Longer Allowed
This used to be a familiar scene. Johnny Miller has just stroked a putt while caddie Andy Martinez crouches behind Miller on an extension of the line of putt. The Rules now prohibit such assistance. The caddie must get off the line before the stroke is made. (R. 35-1e)

d. Conceding Opponent's Next Stroke

When the opponent's ball has come to rest, the player may concede the opponent to have holed out with his next stroke and may remove the opponent's ball with a club or otherwise. If the player does not concede the opponent's next stroke and the opponent's ball fall into the hole, the opponent shall be deemed to have holed out with his last stroke.

If the opponent's next stroke has not been conceded, the opponent shall play without delay in correct order.

Penalty for breach of Rule 35-2: *Loss of hole.*

a. BALL INTERFERING WITH PLAY

When the competitor's ball lies on the putting green, if the competitor consider that a fellow-competitor's ball interfere with his play, he may require that the fellow-competitor's ball be lifted or played, at the fellow-competitor's option.

If a ball be accidentally moved in complying with this Rule, no penalty shall be incurred and the ball shall be replaced.

Note: *It is recommended that the interfering ball be played rather than lifted, unless the subsequent play of a fellow-competitor is likely to be affected.*

b. BALL ASSISTING PLAY

If the fellow-competitor consider that his ball lying on the putting green might be of assistance to the competitor, the fellow-competitor may lift or play first, without penalty.

c. BALL STRIKING FELLOW-COMPETITOR'S BALL

When both balls lie on the putting green, if the competitor's ball strike a fellow-competitor's ball, the *competitor shall incur a penalty of two strokes* and shall play his ball as it lies. The fellow-competitor's ball shall be at once replaced.

d. BALL LIFTED BEFORE HOLED OUT

For ball lifted before holed out, see Rules 7-2, 27-lc and 35-1k.

Rule 35 is by far the longest of the 41 Rules, since it covers that part of the course—the putting green—on which a disproportionate amount of activity is concentrated. Every player and every ball eventually converges on the putting green, where golfers of all levels of skill take something on the order of 35 to 40 percent of their strokes.

Rule 35 is divided into three sections, headed "General," "Match Play" and "Stroke Play." We'll approach them in order.

35-1 General

a—The line of putt is holy ground and it's not to be touched except as specifically allowed in the next three clauses of the Rule. If the line of putt could be touched indiscriminately, it is conceivable that a depression would be developed near the hole from different forms of banging or gardening, so that, in effect, the size of the hole would be increased. There is a tendency to become all too casual about the line of putt. Here are some examples of touching the line of putt that violate Rule 35:

*Repairing spike or scuff marks which, says the USGA, "would be so difficult to define for Rules purposes that a Rule permitting their repair could open the door for repair of any minor imperfection in the putting surface."

*Brushing aside or sopping up casual water. The same goes for dew.

*Deliberately walking across the line of putt, since contact with the feet constitutes a form of touching.

1b—Understand that you can use *only* a club or your hand to pick up or brush aside loose impediments. Thus, it's a violation to use a cap or towel. On the pro tour we feel so strongly about the issue that we employ a Local Rule that doesn't even allow the club to be used.

On the Edge
When a ball hangs on the edge of the hole, the player is allowed only a few seconds to wait for it to fall. After that, it is deemed to be at rest and play must proceed. The USGA says a few seconds is not more than ten. (R.35-1i)

1

2

3

Marking a Ball

When a ball on a putting green is lifted, its position must be marked. I use a coin (1) and place it immediately behind the ball (2) before lifting the ball (3). When the coin interferes with another player, it's moved to one side the length of one or more putterheads. To be sure I can replace the coin exactly where it was, I first pick out a reference point— often a tree (4)—before setting down my putter between the coin and the reference point (5). The last step is to move the coin (6). (R. 35-1k)

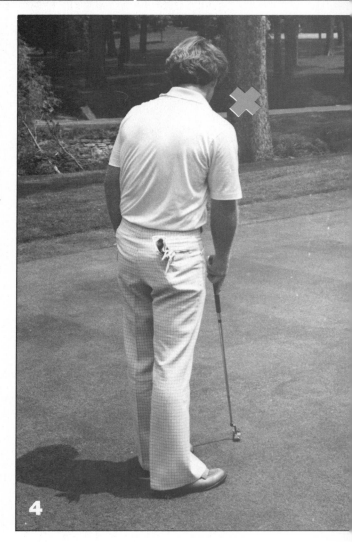

4

1c—Effective in 1980 this clause was liberalized to allow for repair of old hole plugs in addition to ball marks. Note that ball marks on the aprons on your line may not be repaired, since they are not on putting greens. But even though the ball is not on a green, marks on the green may be repaired.

1d—A generous clause. You can mark and lift anytime you desire, including in match play, without awaiting the consent of your opponent. The ball must be replaced in a match, however, if your opponent insists.

1e—This clause is commonly violated when caddies and partners touch the green itself with a club or flagstick while pointing to what they consider to be the line. (The line, by the way, is not necessarily a straight line from ball to hole. The slope of the ground and even error in making the stroke must be considered in resolving any questions about defining the line.) The second part of this clause was

5

6

Sam Snead Then and Now
There was a time when Sam Snead tried to cure his putting problems by straddling the line of putt and making his version of the croquet stroke (1). The Rules of Golf banned standing astride the line of putt beginning in 1968. Sam still uses the croquet-style stroke, but now he putts with his feet together to the side of the line of putt (2). (R. 35-1l)

inserted specifically to stop what was the growing practice of caddies crouching behind players as they prepared to putt to counsel them on the alignment of their putters. The practice was employed by, among others, Johnny Miller and Dave Hill. The USGA and R&A thought the use of a caddie in such a manner altered the nature of the game by making the caddie something more than he should be.

1f—There are two reasons for this clause: It protects the greens from abrasions and it helps to maintain putting as a craft that requires extraordinary sensitivity. If I could rub the surface of greens, it would help me to "read" the grain of the grasses better and make putting somewhat easier. Decision 70-31, in response to a question put by Jerome T. Butwin, of New York City, says: "Cleaning the ball by rubbing it on the surface of the putting green does not violate the Rules provided the act is not for the purpose of testing the surface of the green." The Decision then goes on to recommend that the ball be cleaned in other ways "so as to eliminate questions as to the player's intentions."

1g—An easy one. No one plays or touches another ball while another one is in motion.

1h—Example: A dog bounds onto a green and pounces on a ball while it's still moving. The stroke, if played from a green, must be canceled and replayed. The same applies in stroke play if a ball is accidentally deflected by a fellow-competitor or his caddie, since they are outside agencies in stroke play.

1i—There was a time when golfers used to claim they would violate Rule 25 by tapping in balls which hung on the lip of the hole on the grounds that the ball was moving—ever so slightly. Don January, in fact, waited for seven minutes on the 72nd green of the 1963 Phoenix Open in just such a situation; the ball never fell. The Rule was later changed. What it now says, in effect, is: "Never mind about Rule 25. You are exempt from violating it in this situation. If the ball doesn't fall into the hole after a few seconds, it is at rest no matter what you or anyone else thinks."

OK, so what's a few seconds? The USGA, in a landmark Decision issued after the January incident (66-5), said that a few seconds "is a very short period of time, certainly no more than ten seconds." The imaginary clock begins to tick "when the player reaches or could reach without unreasonable delay, a position enabling him to determine whether his ball is at rest." In match play the opponent *must* allow the player his few seconds before conceding the putt. There was a fascinating violation and application of this Rule on the tour when, during the second round of a Heritage Classic at Hilton Head Island, South Carolina, Grier Jones—who simply didn't know the Rule—allowed his ball to hang on the edge for much longer than a few seconds before the ball fell into the hole. Before the next round started it was learned that the incident had been captured on video tape by CBS, which just happened to be rehearsing on that hole during the second round. The tape clearly showed that Grier waited much longer than the few seconds allowed in Rule 35-1i. Grier was disqualified for having turned in a score lower than he actually made, i.e., he had not included the two-stroke penalty he incurred for delaying play under Rule 37-7. His scorecard showed 3 when it should have been 5. I wonder if this wasn't the only time in any sport that a television replay has ever been used in such a way.

1j—The extent of the drop from a wrong putting green is one club-length. Prior to 1980 it was two club-lengths.

1k—This clause says that it's OK to mark the position of a lifted ball with anything (including a tee or a putterhead) as long as it *is* marked, but the recommended procedure calls for the use of a ball marker to be placed immediately behind the ball. (On the tour we use a Local Rule that mandates the recommended procedure.) If a player fails to mark the position of his ball before lifting it, he incurs a penalty of one stroke, and the ball shall be replaced.

1l—The Rules-makers outlawed straddle-style putting with this Rule in 1968 on the grounds that although the straddlers technically complied with the definition of a stroke, it was a form of stroke contrary to the high traditions and best interests of the game. Moreover, the putters used by straddlers could be perfectly balanced instruments and, in theory anyway, easier to use than a regular putter. Sam Snead and Bob Duden, you may recall, were the primary straddle-style putters. Sam's reaction was to adopt a form of side-straddle putting, which he employs with varying degrees of effectiveness to this day.

35-2 Match Play

2a—A statement of the principle in match play that the player whose ball is away controls his opponent's ball in the sense that he can require the opponent to either leave his ball where it is or lift it.

2b—This restates what Rule 20 said: If the player who is not farther from the hole plays first, the opponent has the option of either allowing the stroke played out of turn to stand or requiring that it be replayed. The only distinction is that if the stroke is to be replayed on the putting green, the ball is replaced; elsewhere on the course it's to be dropped.

2c—In this case it's the opponent who gets to choose. If his ball is moved, he can either replace it or play from where it then lies.

2d—Concessions should be loud and clear. Once a putt is conceded, that's it. The player is considered to have holed out on his next stroke. The concession may not be recalled or declined. In four-ball match play, if a putt has been conceded but the player goes ahead and putts anyway because he hopes to show his partner the correct line, the *partner* should be disqualified from that hole, since he was the intended beneficiary of the act. See Rule 40-3i for an exposition of this principle.

35-3 Stroke Play

3a—When two balls are on the green in stroke play, the competitor whose ball is away can require that the owner of the ball nearer the hole either lift or play—at the option of the competitor whose ball is nearer the hole.

The order of play, the procedure for lifting balls that interfere, and the consequences of striking another ball are different in four-ball play and will be explained after Rules 40 and 41.

3b—A consequence of this clause is vital but somewhat obscure. The impact should come across as a mandate to a competitor whose ball is near the hole and in such a position that it might be helpful to a fellow-competitor who is about to play from off the green. Envision a ball one foot to the side of the hole as another player prepares to blast out of a bunker. The competitor whose ball is near the

Backstop in Match Play

You can use your opponent's ball in a single match (one player versus one player) in this sense: if his ball is next to but just beyond the hole, it might stop yours from rolling by or it might even deflect your ball into the hole. There's no penalty for striking the opponent's ball. (R. 35-2a)

Single Match Rules
Player A has putted, gone by the hole, and struck B's ball. There's no penalty. B has the option of playing his ball as it lies or returning it to its original position. (R. 35-2c)

hole has an *obligation* to the rest of the field to lift his ball. It was expressed this way in Decision 59-8 in reply to a query from a golfer whose ball was in a bunker and wanted to have a fellow-competitor leave his ball, as a potential backstop near the hole:

It is a basic principle of stroke play that one ball shall not assist another. When a fellow-competitor's ball might assist a competitor, the fellow-competitor has an obligation to the rest of the field to exercise the option given him in Rule 35-3b and lift or play first. If a competitor and fellow-competitor were to agree to violate this basic principle, we would invoke Rule 4 and disqualify both.

3c—Again we see the principle that one ball is not to assist another in stroke play—a fundamental difference with match play. There's a two-stroke penalty for hitting another ball on the green with a ball you've putted.

3d—The references reveal that if a player for some reason picks up his ball and fails to hole out, he incurs a one-stroke penalty and must replace the ball. If he plays a stroke from the next tee before doing so, the penalty is disqualification.

RULE 36: THE COMMITTEE (DEF. 9)

RULE 36-1:

CONDITIONS

The Committee shall lay down the conditions under which a competition is to be played.

Certain special rules governing stroke play are so substantially different from those governing match play that combining the two forms of play is not practicable and is not permitted. The results of matches played and the scores returned in these circumstances shall not be accepted.

RULE 36-2:

ORDER AND TIMES OF STARTING

a. GENERAL

The Committee shall arrange the order and times of starting.

b. MATCH PLAY

When a competition is played over an extended period, the Committee shall lay down the limit of time within which each round shall be completed.

When players are allowed to arrange the date of their match within these limits, the Committee should announce that the match must be played at a stated hour on the last day of the period unless the players agree to a prior date.

c. STROKE PLAY

Competitors shall play in couples unless the Committee authorizes play by threes or fours. If there be a single competitor, the Committee shall provide him with a player who shall mark for him, or provide a marker and allow him to compete alone, or allow him to compete with another group.

RULE 36-3:
DECISION OF TIES

The Committee shall announce the manner, day and time for the decision of a halved match or of a tie, whether played on level terms or under handicap.

A halved match shall not be decided by stroke play. A tie in stroke play shall not be decided by a match.

RULE 36-4:
THE COURSE

a. New Holes
New holes should be made on the day on which a stroke competition begins, and at such other times as the Committee considers necessary, provided all competitors in a single round play with each hole cut in the same position.

b. Practice Ground
Where there is no practice ground available outside the area of a competition course, the Committee should lay down the area on which players may practice on any day of a competition, if it is practicable to do so. On any day of a stroke competition, the Committee should not normally permit practice on or to a putting green or from a hazard of the competition course.

c. Course Unplayable
If the Committee or its authorized representative consider that for any reason the course is not in a playable condition, or that there are circumstances which render the proper playing of the game impossible, it shall have the power in match and stroke play to order a temporary suspension of play, or in stroke play to declare play null and void and to cancel all scores for the round in question.

When a round is cancelled, all penalties incurred in that round are cancelled.

When play has been temporarily suspended, it shall be resumed from where it was discontinued, even though resumption occur on a subsequent day.

(Procedure in discontinuing play—Rule 37-6b.)

RULE 36-5:
MODIFICATION OF PENALTY

The Committee has no power to waive a Rule of Golf. A penalty of disqualification, however, may, in exceptional individual cases, be waived or be modified or be imposed if the Committee consider such action warranted.

RULE 36-6:
DEFINING BOUNDS AND MARGINS

The Committee shall define accurately:—
a. The course and out of bounds.
b. The margins of water hazards and lateral water hazards.
c. Ground under repair.
d. Obstructions.

a. POLICY

The Committee shall make and publish Local Rules for abnormal conditions, having regard to the policy of the Governing Authority of the country concerned as set forth in Appendix I attached to these Rules.

b. WAIVING PENALTY PROHIBITED

A penalty imposed by a Rule of Golf shall not be waived by a Local Rule.

Rule 36 is addressed to those in charge of a competition—the Committee—rather than to the player, but it behooves every golfer to know what Rule 36 is all about. Those who serve on Committees at any level of play should know Rule 36 inside out. Here's an analysis of each part of Rule 36.

1. The conditions should be spelled out in the finest detail. They include the form of play, who is eligible to enter, the number of players in the field, the schedule of rounds and prizes.

The second paragraph points out that match and stroke play are like oil and water. Golfers nevertheless go right on attempting to play matches during a stroke-play round. They run up against conflicts such as the elementary one that occurs when a ball is close to the hole and in position to serve as a helpful backboard. If it's a match, the man about to play is entitled to have the ball left where it is; if it's stroke play, he risks a two-stroke penalty if he hits the ball left on the green. The mix simply doesn't work.

2. Club match-play competitions are often fouled up by a failure of Committees to specify and enforce time limits for the play of rounds. The inability or unwillingness of opponents to get together for a match can spoil a tournament. One way to forestall such a delay is to *assign starting times* in advance to every match in every round but to allow any match to be played at another time, or even on another day, provided the match is completed prior to the schedule set for the next round.

3. Committees seem particularly prone to neglect revealing in advance what's going to happen in the event of a tie. Whenever they forget to do so, someone is invariably unhappy because the method selected, after the fact, always seems to favor someone else.

4. It's a basic principle of stroke play that the course should be the same for the entire field. When something goes wrong and tee markers are moved or the locations of holes are changed during a round, generally the round should be canceled.

The Committee's powers and limitations with respect to suspending play or canceling a round are spelled out in Rule 36-4c:

Match play. All a Committee can do is suspend play and decide when play is to be resumed. Once a match starts and the course becomes unplayable, the results of the holes played before suspension of play are to stand as recorded. The match is *never* begun anew on the first tee.

Stroke play. The Committee can, at its discretion, either cancel an entire round or rule that play is to be resumed where it was discontinued—even on a later day. As a general rule of thumb, the USGA thinks that it's reasonable for a Committee to cancel an entire round when less than half the field completes or could complete play on the day in question.

5. A couple of examples of what this Rule means:

*A player marks his ball one putter-head length to the side, forgets to return the ball to its original position and holes out. When the incident comes to the attention of the Committee, some members might feel that the two-stroke penalty called for in Rule 21-3c for such a violation is unreasonably harsh. Instead, they either assess no penalty or reduce it to one stroke. If the Committee does either, it acts contrary to the Rules of Golf, since a two-stroke penalty may not be waived or modified.

*A player misses his tee time because his ride to the course was delayed by an accident at a railway crossing. The penalty calls for disqualification, but the Committee can waive the penalty or modify it—perhaps to two strokes in stroke play. Mind, the Committee doesn't *have* to do either.

6. We all recognize that it's difficult for Committees to keep courses marked properly for everyday play—particularly with respect to the margins of water hazards and ground under repair—but the effort should be made.

When water hazards are not defined, and the players have to sort things out for themselves, they should bear in mind that the natural limit of the hazard is considered the spot where the ground breaks down to form the depression containing the water. That's where lines and stakes defining the limits of water hazards should normally be placed.

7. Before any round, the wise golfer will check the back of the scorecard and any other likely place, such as a bulletin board, for the posting of Local Rules. A Committee should not impose Local Rules contrary to the Rules of Golf. One bad example would be a Local Rule reading "spike marks may be repaired."

RULE 37: THE PLAYER

RULE 37-1:

CONDITIONS

> The player shall be responsible for acquainting himself with the conditions under which the competition is to be played.

RULE 37-2:

CADDIE

> For any breach of a Rule or Local Rule by his caddie, the player incurs the relative penalty.
>
> The player may have only one caddie, *under penalty of disqualification.*
>
> The player may send his own caddie forward to mark the position of any ball.

RULE 37-3:

FORECADDIE

> If a forecaddie be employed by the Committee, he is an outside agency (Def. 22).

RULE 37-4:

HANDICAP

Before starting in a handicap competition, the player shall ensure that his current handicap is recorded correctly on the official list, if any, for the competition and on the card issued for him by the Committee. In the case of match play or bogey, par or Stableford competitions, he shall inform himself of the holes at which strokes are given or taken.

If a player play off a higher handicap than his current one, *he shall be disqualified* from the handicap competition. If he play off a lower one, the score, or the result of the match, shall stand.

RULE 37-5:

TIME AND ORDER OF STARTING

The player shall start at the time and in the order arranged by the Committee.

PENALTY FOR BREACH OF RULE 37-5: *Disqualification.*

RULE 37-6:

DISCONTINUANCE OF PLAY

a. WHEN PERMITTED

The player shall not discontinue play on account of bad weather or for any other reason, unless:—

He considers that there be danger from lightning,

or

There be some other reason, such as sudden illness, which the Committee considers satisfactory.

If the player discontinue play without specific permission from the Committee, he shall report to the Committee as soon as possible.

General Exception:—Players discontinuing match play by agreement are not subject to disqualification unless by so doing the competition is delayed.

PENALTY FOR BREACH OF RULE 37-6a: *Disqualification.*

b. PROCEDURE

When play is discontinued in accordance with the Rules, it should, if feasible, be discontinued after the completion of the play of a hole. If this is not feasible, the player should lift his ball after marking the spot on which it lay; in such case he shall place a ball on that spot when play is resumed.

PENALTY FOR BREACH OF RULE 37-6b:

*Match play—Loss of hole; *Stroke play—Two strokes.*

***Note:** In stroke play, in the event of a serious breach of Rule 37-6b, see Rules 21-3c and 21-3d.*

RULE 37-7:

UNDUE DELAY

The player shall at all times play without undue delay. Between the completion of a hole and driving off the next tee, the player may not delay play in any way.

PENALTY FOR BREACH OF RULE 37-7:

**Match play—Loss of hole; Stroke play—Two strokes.*

(continued)

151

> *For repeated offense—Disqualification.*
> **If the player delay play between holes, he is delaying the play of the next hole, and the penalty applies to that hole.*

RULE 37-8:

REFUSAL TO COMPLY WITH RULE

> If a competitor in stroke play refuse to comply with a Rule affecting the rights of another competitor, *he shall be disqualified.*

RULE 37-9:

ARTIFICIAL DEVICES

> Except as provided for under the Rules, the player shall not use any artificial device:—
> a. Which might assist him in making a stroke or in his play;
> b. For the purpose of gauging or measuring distance or conditions which might affect his play, or
> c. Which, not being part of the grip (see Appendix IId), is designed to give him artificial aid in gripping the club.
> (*Exceptions to Rule 37-9c:* Plain gloves and material or substance applied to the grip, such as tape, gauze or resin.)
> PENALTY FOR BREACH OF RULE 37-9: *Disqualification.*

Rule 37 contains a potpourri of items that deserve to be in the Rules somewhere and might as well go in here.

While it is up to the Committee to issue scorecards on which handicaps appear, the obligations of Committees and players with respect to handicaps are critical. It is the responsibility of the player to see to it that the handicap on that card *is correct.* Let's say that the Committee makes an error in transcribing a handicap from the official handicap list. If a player goes out to play with a handicap *higher* than that to which he is entitled, the player should be disqualified, whether or not the problem originated in an error by the Committee.

The dictum about handicaps is so stern—and rightly so—that Decision 55-37 called for the disqualification of a team that had won a four-ball match on the day after it was learned that one of the players on the winning side had played with an incorrect handicap. It was reasoned that playing with a too high handicap is tantamount to giving "wrong information."

Discontinuing play, the subject of Rule 37-6, is often a touchy question in club match play when one player or team wants to stop and the other wants to continue. If a Committee has not suspended play in a storm without lightning, the side that wants to forge on has the right to do so. Do, however, note the General Exception to the effect that in match play opponents can by mutual agreement suspend play, *provided* that they don't cause the competition to be delayed.

Lightning is, of course, bad news. Rule 37-6a gives the player the right to stop when "he considers that there be danger from lightning." He doesn't have to consult with his opponents, fellow-competitors or the Committee. Just as I was about to begin the second round of the 1975 Open at Medinah, near Chicago, I saw lightning and heard a clap of thunder. I turned right around and went back into the clubhouse, even though the USGA siren announcing suspension of play had not yet sounded.

One week later, during the Western Open, Lee Trevino, Jerry Heard and Bobby Nichols were all hurt when a bolt of lightning struck near to the spot they were using as an improvised shelter while play was suspended. Every year golfers are killed by lightning and it's impossible to be overly cautious.

The best way to illustrate Rule 37-9 about artificial devices is to present a summary of Decisions:

Not artificial devices. Using weighted head covers; wearing regular eyeglasses; dropping a handkerchief to determine wind conditions; applying gauze tape or wrapping a handkerchief around the grip to keep from slipping; using a booklet illustrating distances to holes from various landmarks; using a hand warmer, provided it is not also used to affect the temperature of golf balls.

Artificial devices. Using any of the following: field glasses which have a range-finder feature; an actual plumb line—a weight suspended from a string; a ball warmer during a round; an electronic instrument used to find balls which have transmitters embedded in their cores.

RULE 38: SCORING IN STROKE PLAY

RULE 38-1:

RECORDING SCORES

The Committee shall issue for each competitor a score card containing the date and the competitor's name.

After each hole the marker should check the score with the competitor. On completion of the round the marker shall sign the card and hand it to the competitor; should more than one marker record the scores, each shall sign the part for which he is responsible.

RULE 38-2:

CHECKING SCORES

The competitor shall check his score for each hole, settle any doubtful points with the Committee, ensure that the marker has signed the card, countersign the card himself, and return it to the Committee as soon as possible. The competitor is solely responsible for the correctness of the score recorded for each hole.

PENALTY FOR BREACH OF RULE 38-2: *Disqualification.*

The Committee is responsible for the addition of scores and application of the handicap recorded on the card.

Exception: Four-ball stroke play—Rule 41-1d.

RULE 38-3:

NO ALTERATION OF SCORES

No alteration may be made on a card after the competitor has returned it to the Committee.

If the competitor return a score for any hole lower than

(continued)

> actually taken, *he shall be disqualified.*
> A score higher than actually taken must stand as re-
> turned.
> *Exception:*—Four-ball stroke play—Rule 41-8a.

Rule 38 is limited to stroke play because scoring in match play depends entirely on the opponents' agreement or understanding as to the status of the match. It's a sound principle that a scorecard be kept during a match, but the card itself has no official status and it need not be signed or turned in. All that's required is that the result be presented to the Committee.

As for stroke play, I suppose the application of Rule 38 has prompted some of the most celebrated Rules of Golf controversies in the history of the game. Roberto deVicenzo should have tied Bob Goalby for first in the 1968 Masters and played off the next day, but Roberto, who had made a birdie 3 on the 17th hole, countersigned the card prepared by Tommy Aaron, his marker, which erroneously showed "4" in the box for the 17th hole. According to Rule 38-3, the higher score had to stand and the one-stroke difference made Roberto the runner-up.

Back in 1957, there was a similarly unhappy incident when Jackie Pung was disqualified from the Women's Open Championship because she countersigned a card that had her making a 5 at the 4th hole, where she had actually made a 6. The total on the card was correct. A simple error of transposition had been made by her marker. Mrs. Pung's card should have read "5-6" for two successive holes, but instead it read "6-5."

There was an uproar after both cases. The USGA, in fact, issued a general invitation after the deVicenzo incident for submissions of improved versions of the scoring Rule. But nothing that was submitted seemed to improve it.

Personally, I'll take Rule 38 just the way it is. It gives me the absolute right to be responsible for my score. I don't have to counter-sign the card until and unless I'm satisfied with what it shows. Any alteration in Rule 38 would erode that privilege.

The marker in tour events is always another player in the same group. A scorer accompanies each group. The card the scorer maintains is the source of scores for the scoreboards and the media. As soon as I finish, I always double-check my scorecard by first circling and checking my birdies and bogeys and then going over the card hole by hole with the unofficial scorer.

Actually, the most common cause for disqualification under Rule 38 is forgetting to sign the card. That's the first and last thing I think about in the scoring tent. So far I've never been disqualified for turning in an incorrect card or failing to sign one.

RULE 39: BOGEY, PAR OR STABLEFORD COMPETITIONS

RULE 39-1:
———————
CONDITIONS

> A bogey, par or Stableford competition is a form of stroke competition in which play is against a fixed score at each
>
> *(continued)*

hole of the stipulated round or rounds.

a. The reckoning for bogey or par competitions is made as in match play. The winner is the competitor who is most successful in the aggregate of holes.

b. The reckoning in Stableford competitions is made by points awarded in relation to a fixed score at each hole as follows:—

For hole done in one over fixed score—1 point
For hole done in fixed score—2 points
For hole done in one under fixed score—3 points
For hole done in two under fixed score—4 points
For hole done in three under fixed score—5 points

The winner is the competitor who scores the highest number of points.

RULE 39-2:

RULES FOR STROKE PLAY APPLY

The Rules for stroke play shall apply with the following modifications:—

a. No RETURN AT ANY HOLE

Any hole for which a competitor makes no return shall be regarded as a loss in bogey and par competitions and as scoring no points in Stableford competitions.

b. SCORING CARDS

The holes at which strokes are to be given or taken shall be indicated on the card issued by the Committee.

c. RECORDING SCORES

In bogey and par competitions the marker shall be responsible for marking only the gross number of strokes for each hole where the competitor makes a net score equal to or less than the fixed score. In Stableford competitions the marker shall be responsible for marking only the gross number of strokes at each hole where the competitor's net score earns one or more points. **Note:** *Maximum of 14 Clubs—see Rule 3-2 and Rule 41-7.*

RULE 39-3:

DISQUALIFICATION PENALTIES

a. FROM THE COMPETITION

A competitor shall be disqualified from the competition for a breach of any of the following:

Rule 2—The Club and the Ball.
Rule 4—Agreement to Waive Rules Prohibited.
Rule 8-3—Practice before Round.
Rule 35-3a—Putting Green: Stroke Play, Ball Interfering with Play.
Rule 37-2—Caddie.
Rule 37-4—Handicap (playing off higher handicap than current one).
Rule 37-5—Time and Order of Starting.
Rule 37-6a—Discontinuance of Play.
Rule 37-7—Undue Delay (repeated offense).

(continued)

Rule 37-8—Refusal to Comply with Rule.
Rule 37-9—Artificial Devices.
Rule 38-2—Checking Scores.
Rule 38-3—No Alteration of Scores, except that the competitor shall not be disqualified when a breach of this Rule does not affect the result of the hole.

b. FOR A HOLE
In all other cases where a breach of a Rule would entail disqualification, *the competitor shall be disqualified only for the hole at which the breach occurred.*
(*Modification of penalty*—Rule 36-5.)

Rule 39 sets down the conditions for some forms of competition which offer a form of relief from the routine of standard stroke play.

Bogey or Par competitions are played against a fixed score. The most popular method calls for the par on each hole to serve as the opponent. A player is up against par but with the help of a handicap. The winner is the player who is most ahead of par after eighteen holes.

Stableford competitions are indigenous to Great Britain. They're often called "point" tournaments here. They're a lot of fun because they allow players of every level of skill to play, suffer and exult together. A common form of Stableford sends out teams of four, each player using full handicap. A net score of a double bogey, or worse, for a player earns no points on a hole, but a bogey is worth 1 point, a par 2 points and so on up to 5 points on a hole for a net double eagle. The winning team is the one which amasses the most total points: every 2-foot putt for a net bogey takes on a meaning all its own.

Stableford, in case you're interested, was Dr. Frank B. Stableford of Great Britain, a surgeon and first-rate golfer who invented the scoring system that bears his name. History records that the first Stableford tournament was played on May 16, 1932, on the Wallasey Links, Cheshire, England.

RULE 40: THREE-BALL, BEST-BALL AND FOUR-BALL MATCH PLAY

RULE 40-1:

GENERAL

a. RULES OF GOLF APPLY
The Rules of Golf, so far as they are not at variance with the following special Rules, shall apply to all three-ball, best-ball and four-ball matches.

b. BALL INFLUENCING PLAY
Any player may have any ball (except the ball about to be played) lifted if he consider that it might interfere with or be of assistance to a player or side, but this may not be done while any ball in the match is in motion.

c. BALL MOVED BY ANOTHER BALL
There is no penalty if a player's ball move any other ball in the match. The owner of the moved ball shall replace his ball.

d. PLAYING OUT OF TURN   *(continued)*

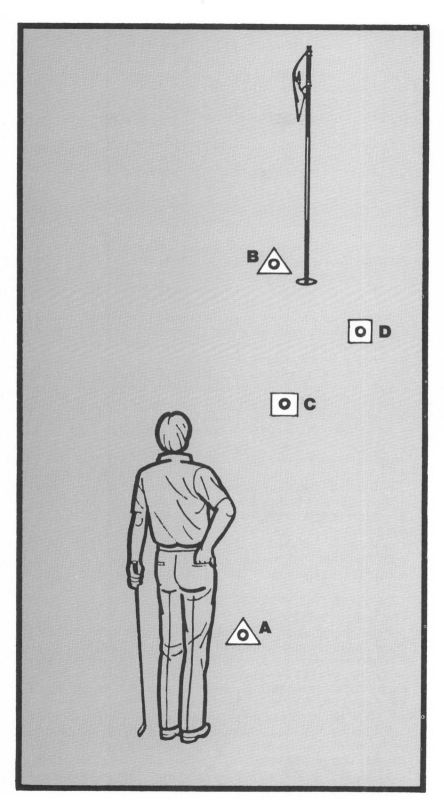

Four-Ball Match Play

The control of the balls in a four-ball match (two players against two players) is different than in a single match or in stroke play. In a four-ball match, any *player can have* any *ball lifted before a stroke is made. In this illustration, A and B are partners and it's A's turn to putt. He'll obviously require that C's ball be lifted, since it's on his line. A would probably like B's ball to stay right where it is, since it could serve as a useful backstop, but either C or D can require B to lift his ball. As for ball D, it's off the line of putt, but A can have it lifted if it bothers him. If any ball is not lifted and is struck by ball A, there is no penalty. A would play from where his ball then lies, while the owner of the displaced ball, whether he's A's partner or opponent, must replace it. (R. 40-1b and R. 40-1c)*

On the teeing ground, if a player play when an opponent should have played, the opponent may immediately require the player to abandon the ball so played and to play a ball in correct order, without penalty.

Through the green or in a hazard, a player shall incur no penalty if he play when an opponent should have done so. The stroke shall not be replayed.

On the putting green, if a player play when an opponent should have done so, the opponent may immediately require the player to replay the stroke in correct order, without penalty.

RULE 40-2:
THREE-BALL MATCH PLAY

In a three-ball match, each player is playing two distinct matches.

a. BALL STOPPED OR DEFLECTED BY AN OPPONENT ACCIDENTALLY

If a player's ball be accidentally stopped or deflected by an opponent, his caddie or equipment, no penalty shall be incurred. In his match with that opponent, the player may play the ball as it lies or, before another stroke is played by either side, he may cancel the stroke, place a ball on the spot where the ball previously lay and replay the stroke. In his match with the other opponent, the occurrence shall be treated as a rub of the green (Def. 27) and the hole shall be played out with the original ball.

Exception:—Ball striking person attending flagstick—Rule 34-3b.

(Ball purposely stopped or deflected by opponent—Rule 17-4.)

b. BALL AT REST MOVED BY AN OPPONENT

If the player's ball be touched or moved by an opponent, his caddie or equipment (except as otherwise provided in the Rules), Rule 27-2a applies. *That opponent shall incur a penalty stroke in his match with the player,* but not in his match with the other opponent.

RULE 40-3:
BEST-BALL AND FOUR-BALL MATCH PLAY

a. ORDER OF PLAY

Balls belonging to the same side may be played in the order the side considers best.

b. BALL STOPPED BY PLAYER'S SIDE

If a player's ball be stopped or deflected by the player, his partner or either of their caddies or equipment, *the player is disqualified for the hole.* His partner incurs no penalty.

c. BALL STOPPED BY OPPONENT'S SIDE ACCIDENTALLY

If a player's ball be accidentally stopped or deflected by an opponent, his caddie or equipment, no penalty shall be incurred. The player may play the ball as it lies or, before

(continued)

another stroke is played by either side, he may cancel the stroke, place a ball on the spot where the ball previously lay and replay the stroke.

Exception:—Ball striking person attending flagstick—Rule 34-3b.

(Ball purposely stopped or deflected by opponent—Rule 17-4.)

d. WRONG BALL

If a player play a stroke with a wrong ball (Def. 5) except in a hazard, *he shall be disqualified for that hole,* but the penalty shall not apply to his partner. If the wrong ball belong to another player, its owner shall place a ball on the spot from which the wrong ball was played, without penalty.

e. PARTNER'S BALL MOVED BY PLAYER ACCIDENTALLY

If a player, his partner, or either of their caddies accidentally move a ball owned by their side or by touching anything cause it to move (except as otherwise provided for in the Rules), *the owner of the ball shall incur a penalty stroke,* but the penalty shall not apply to his partner. The ball shall be replaced.

f. BALL MOVED BY OPPONENT'S SIDE

If a player's ball be touched or moved by an opponent, his caddie or equipment (except as otherwise provided for in the Rules), *that opponent shall incur a penalty stroke,* but the penalty shall not apply to the other opponent. The player shall replace the ball, without penalty.

g. MAXIMUM OF FOURTEEN CLUBS

The side shall be penalized for a violation of Rule 3 by either partner.

h. DISQUALIFICATION PENALTIES

A player shall be disqualified from the match for a breach of Rule 37-5 (Time and Order of Starting), but, in the discretion of the Committee, the penalty shall not necessarily apply to his partner (Definition 28—Note).

A side shall be disqualified for a breach of any of the following:—

Rule 2—The Club and the Ball.

Rule 4—Agreement to Waive Rules Prohibited.

Rule 37-2—Caddie.

Rule 37-4—Handicap (playing off higher handicap than current one).

Rule 37-7—Undue Delay (repeated offense).

Rule 37-9—Artificial Devices.

A player shall be disqualified for the hole in question and from the remainder of the match for a breach of Rule 37-6a (Discontinuance of Play), but the penalty shall not apply to his partner.

(Modification of penalty—Rule 36-5.)

i. INFRINGEMENT ASSISTING PARTNER OR AFFECTING OPPONENT

If a player's infringement of a Rule or Local Rule assist his partner's play or adversely affect an opponent's play, *the partner incurs the relative penalty in addition to any penalty incurred by the player.* *(continued)*

j. PENALTY APPLIES TO PLAYER ONLY

In all other cases where, by the Rules or Local Rules, a player would incur a penalty, the penalty shall not apply to his partner.

k. ANOTHER FORM OF MATCH PLAYED CONCURRENTLY

In a best-ball or a four-ball match when another form of match is played concurrently, the above special Rules shall apply.

The most popular form of play is undoubtedly four-ball match play, which consists of two playing their better ball on each hole against the better ball of two others.

Rule 40 also covers Best-Ball (when one player goes up against the best ball of either two or three others) and Three-Ball (when three play against one another, each playing his own ball.) But these two forms of play are so rare that we'll skip them and concentrate on four-ball match play.

Let's go right to the site of common confusion—on the putting green, where the Rules are markedly different for lifting balls in the various forms of play.

In a four-ball match, good old A and B are up against C and D.

Case 1: A is away and B's ball is inches beyond the hole in such a position that it might very well assist A as a backstop. A would like B's ball to stay right where it is, but Rule 40-1b gives C and D the right to require that B's ball be lifted.

Case 2: This time B's ball is directly in front of the hole on A's line. Naturally, A and B want B's ball lifted and they may do so.

Case 3: Now picture C's ball just beyond the hole where it might help A. C can mark and lift his ball. (In a single match, C would not have been in control.)

Case 4: C's ball is on A's line. A can require him to lift it.

Let's assume, however, that in each case no ball is marked, that A putts and strikes the ball of either B, his partner, or C, his opponent. There is no penalty. A plays from where his ball then lies. The owner of the ball moved, be it partner or opponent, must replace his ball.

Singles matches are often played concurrently with the four-ball match. Thus A and B are not only going up against the team of C and D, but A is waging singles matches at the same time against C and D, and sometimes even against partner B. What to do when the procedure for four-ball match play is at variance with these for single matches? Easy. The four-ball rules have priority! It says so loud and clear in Rule 40-3k.

Let's again consider the common situation where A is away and the ball of one of his opponents', Mr. C, might very well be of assistance. The principle in a single match was that A, being away, "controls" C's ball. Forget that principle in a four-ball match! C may lift his ball.

Some other key elements in four-ball matches:

*Rule 40-3a introduces a strategic possibility in that even though A is away, his partner—Dr. B—may play first. Then it's A's turn.

*When your ball is deflected by your partner, caddie or equipment (including a cart you may be sharing), you are disqualified for that hole, but he plays on.

*When your ball is accidentally deflected by one of your opponents, their caddies or their equipment, there is no penalty. You have a choice of either playing your ball as it lies or replaying the stroke. This represents a change in Rule 40-3c introduced in 1980.

*When a player violates a Rule, his partner is not penalized *unless* the nature of the violation is such that it helps his partner or hurts the play of an opponent. When that happens, both members of the team are penalized. Example: After balls have been lifted and replaced on a putting green, A makes a mistake and putts from the spot where B's marker was. The putt is a tricky downhiller, with a big right-to-left break. A, having played from a wrong place, is disqualified on that hole, and B, since he might very well have been assisted by observing the roll of the ball, should also be disqualified.

RULE 41: FOUR-BALL STROKE PLAY

RULE 41-1:

CONDITIONS

a. The Rules of Golf, so far as they are not at variance with the following special Rules, shall apply to four-ball stroke play.

b. In four-ball stroke play two competitors play as partners, each playing his own ball.

c. The lower score of the partners is the score of the hole. If one partner fail to complete the play of a hole, there is no penalty.

(Wrong score—Rule 41-8a.)

d. The marker is required to record for each hole only the gross score of whichever partner's score is to count. The partners are responsible for the correctness of only their gross scores for each hole. The Committee is responsible for recording the better-ball score for each hole, the addition and the application of the handicaps recorded on the card.

e. Only one of the partners need be responsible for complying with Rule 38.

RULE 41-2:

BALL INFLUENCING PLAY

Any competitor may have any ball (except the ball about to be played) lifted or played, at the option of the owner, if he consider that it might interfere with or be of assistance to a competitor or side, but this may not be done while any ball in the group is in motion.

If the owner of the ball refuse to comply with this Rule when required to do so, *his side shall be disqualified.*

RULE 41-3:

BALLS TO BE AT REST

While the competitor's ball is in motion after a stroke on the putting green, any other ball shall not be played or touched.

When the balls concerned lie on the putting green, if a competitor's ball strike any other ball, *the competitor shall incur a penalty of two strokes* and shall play his ball as it lies. The other ball shall be at once replaced.

In all other cases, if a competitor's ball strike any other ball, the competitor shall play his ball as it lies. The owner of the moved ball shall replace his ball, without penalty.

Balls belonging to the same side may be played in the order the side considers best.

If a competitor play any strokes with a wrong ball (Def. 5) except in a hazard, *he shall add two penalty strokes* to his score for the hole and then play the correct ball (Rule 21-3).

If the wrong ball belong to another player its owner shall place a ball on the spot from which the wrong ball was played, without penalty.

The side shall be penalized for a violation of Rule 3 by either partner.

a. From the Competition
A competitor shall be disqualified from the competition for a breach of any of the following, but the penalty shall not apply to his partner:—
    Rule 8-3—Practice before Round.
    Rule 37-5—Time and Order of Starting.
A side shall be disqualified from the competition for a breach of any of the following:—
    Rule 2—The Club and the Ball.
    Rule 4—Agreement to Waive Rules Prohibited.
    Rule 37-2—Caddie.
    Rule 37-4—Handicap (playing off higher handicap than current one).
    Rule 37-7—Undue Delay (repeated offense).
    Rule 37-8—Refusal to Comply with Rule.
    Rule 37-9—Artificial Devices.
    Rule 38-2—Checking Scores.
    Rule 38-3—No alteration of scores, i.e., when the recorded lower score of the partners is lower than actually played. If the recorded lower score of the partners is higher than actually played, it must stand as returned.
    Rule 41-2—Ball Influencing Play, Refusal to Lift.

(continued)

By both partners, at the same hole, of a Rule or Rules the penalty for which is disqualification either from the competition or for a hole.

b. FROM THE REMAINDER OF THE COMPETITION

A competitor shall be disqualified for the hole in question and from the remainder of the competition for a breach of Rule 37-6a (Discontinuance of Play), *but the penalty shall not apply to his partner.*

c. FOR THE HOLE ONLY

In all other cases where a breach of a Rule would entail disqualification, *the competitor shall be disqualified only for the hole at which the breach occurred.*

(Modification of penalty—Rule 36-5.)

RULE 41-9:

INFRINGEMENT ASSISTING PARTNER

If a competitor's infringement of a Rule or Local Rule assist his partner's play, *the partner incurs the relative penalty in addition to any penalty incurred by the competitor.*

RULE 41-10:

PENALTY APPLIES TO COMPETITOR ONLY

In all other cases where, by the Rules or Local Rules, a competitor would incur a penalty, the penalty shall not apply to his partner.

The Rules governing four-ball stroke and match play vary when a ball is moved by another ball. When a ball is putted and strikes another ball in four-ball stroke play, the player who putted is penalized two strokes. The moved ball must be replaced.

Partners in four-ball stroke play may not "use" each other's balls as potential backstops. If A is about to play from a bunker and the ball of partner B is just beyond the hole, B's ball should be removed.

Rule 41 is customarily adopted to control best-ball-of-four competitions—those in which each four-man team counts the best score on a hole as the team score for the hole. Another standard variation is the pro-amateur format which finds the pro recording his score on each hole (since he's playing a stroke play competition against the other pros in the field) while at the same time he and his amateur partners are engaged in a best-ball-of-four (or even five) competition.

LOCAL RULES

It is the responsibility of the Committee to decide whether it's necessary to make Local Rules, but such Local Rules should not be contrary to the Rules of Golf.

Local Rules customarily appear on the reverse sides of scorecards and are often supplemented by notices posted on bulletin boards or near the first tee.

Appendix I following the Rules of Golf says that the following are "among the matters for which Local Rules or other regulations may be advisable":

1. Lateral Water Hazards
Clarifying the status of sections of water hazards which may be lateral under Definition 14c and Rule 33-3.

2. Obstructions
a. CLARIFYING STATUS: Clarifying the status of objects which may be obstructions under Definition 20 and Rule 31.

b. WHEN INTEGRAL PART OF COURSE: Declaring not an obstruction any construction which the Committee considers an integral part of the course (Definition 20c); e.g., built-up sides and surfaces of teeing grounds, putting greens and bunkers.

3. Defining Bounds and Margins
Specifying means used to define out of bounds, hazards, water hazards, lateral water hazards, and ground under repair.

4. Ball Drops
Establishment of special areas on which balls may be dropped when it is not feasible to proceed exactly in conformity with Rule 29-2b (ball unplayable), Rule 31-2b (immovable obstruction) and Rules 33-2, -3 (water hazards and lateral water hazards).

5. Provisional Ball, Water Hazard
Permitting play of a provisional ball for a ball which may be in a water hazard of such character that it would be impracticable to determine whether the ball is in the hazard or to do so would unduly delay play. In such case, if a provisional ball is played and the original ball is in a water hazard, the player may play the original ball as it lies or continue the provisional ball in play, but he may not proceed under Rule 33-2 or 33-3.

6. Preservation of Course
Preservation of the course, including turf nurseries and other parts of the course under cultivation on which play is prohibited.

7. Temporary Conditions—Mud, Extreme Wetness
Temporary conditions which might interfere with proper playing of the game, including mud and extreme wetness warranting lifting an embedded ball anywhere through the green on specific individual days *(see detailed recommendation below)* or removal of mud from a ball through the green.

8. Accumulation of Leaves
9. Unusual Damage To the Course
(other than as covered in Rule 32.)

10. Roads and Paths
Providing relief of the type afforded under Rule 31-2b from roads and paths not having artificial surfaces and sides if they could unfairly affect play.

11. Priority On the Course (see Etiquette)
12. Practice Areas (see Rules 8 and 36-4b)
13. Automotive Transport
Specifying whether automotive transportation may or may not be used by players.

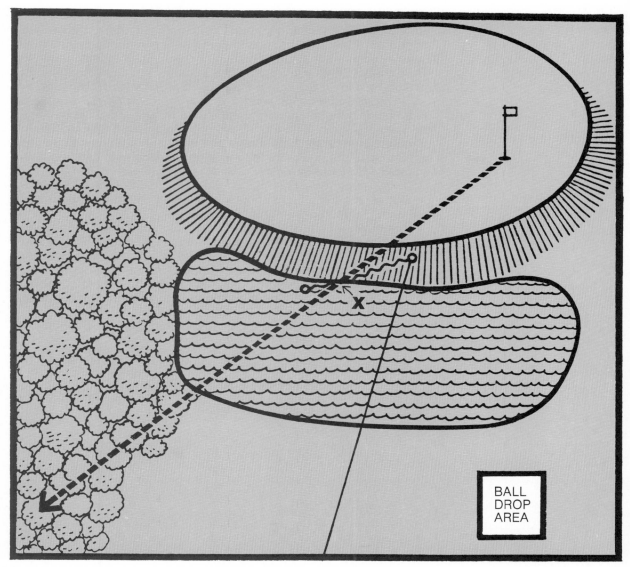

BALL
DROP
AREA

Ball-Drop Area

Committees can install special ball-drop areas when it's not practical or unfair to limit players to the standard water-hazard options. Take this hole, which has a pond directly in front of the green and a slope between the pond and the elevated green. Balls often carry beyond the hazard into the slope but then carom back into the hazard. Often dropping behind the point where the ball last entered the hazard (X) on an extension of a line between the point and the hole means the player would have to drop into a veritable jungle—not a very desirable option. The stroke-and-distance option, of course, is always available, but that may seem too severe. So the Committee installs a clearly defined ball-drop area (lower right), which the player may use for the customary penalty of one stroke. (R. 33-1 and Local Rules)

Appendix I also suggests the text for a Local Rule authorizing lifting embedded balls "through the green" when a Committee feels that it would be unfair to confine the lifting of embedded balls to the putting green (see Rule 35-1c) and other closely mown areas (see Rule 16-2). Unless a more generous Local Rule is in effect, balls that are embedded in the rough may not be lifted without penalty.

"Preferred Lies" and "Winter Rules," which allow for moving the ball contrary to the principle expressed in Rule 16: "the ball shall be played as it lies," are also a subject in Appendix I. The USGA says it does not endorse such Rules and will not interpret them, and points out quite correctly that they do fundamental damage to the principle that the ball should be played as it lies.

At the same time, it is recognized that conditions are sometimes so harsh that it's not possible to have a decent game without some form of "Preferred Lies" or "Winter Rules."

It is essential that this condition by covered by a detailed Local Rule. A notice posted only with the wording "Winter Rules" doesn't do the job. It suggests that the lie of the ball may be improved, but it doesn't answer the fundamental questions:

*May the lie of the ball be improved only in the fairway of the hole being played, on any fairway, through the green, or in hazards—or sections of some hazards?

*When the ball is moved, may it be lifted, and if so, cleaned, or must it be moved only with a club head?

*How far may the ball be moved—six inches, one club-length, two club-lengths?

*When is the ball in play? Is it, for instance, in play as soon as it has been placed or is not in play until the player makes his next stroke?

RULES OF GOLF QUIZ

So now you know it all! You've plowed through my admonitions on Etiquette, the thirty-six Definitions, the forty-one Rules and Local Rules. If there is one thing I am sure of, it is that you are a truly concerned golfer. Congratulations! If golf had more people like you, it would be a better game for all of us.

I hope you have enjoyed your labors and have profited from them. For your final exam I have included a quiz originally devised by P. J. Boatwright, Jr., to test the skills of a group of golf association executives attending a conference. It's meant to test your ability to *use* this book rather than your ability to snap off the correct answers. It's very much an open-book test, and each and every answer is readily available within the Rules proper. That is to say, it's not necessary for you to have memorized the Rules of Golf and have a 100 percent ability to recall the gist of Decisions on the Rules in order to answer Mr. Boatwright's questions.

The best way to join in the challenge of this quiz is to try to answer as many questions as possible within thirty minutes.

It is not intended to be an easy quiz. Anything but! If you can answer 40 of the 50 questions correctly within the thirty minutes, you're not far from being an expert. Anything better than that and you are one already! Good luck, and thanks for being an interested student.

The answers to the quiz appear on page 177.

1. A player's ball comes to rest against a sprinkler head. He drops the ball one club-length from the sprinkler head under Rule 31-2. The ball rolls two club-lengths after being dropped, so that it is almost three club-lengths from the sprinkler head. What is the proper procedure for the player?

_____(a) He must re-drop the ball as it lies more than two club-lengths from the sprinkler head.

_____(b) The ball is in play and he must play it as it lies.

_____(c) He has the option of playing the ball as it lies or re-dropping.

2. A player's ball lies in a lateral water hazard. He wishes to drop the ball 30 yards behind the hazard under penalty of one stroke, keeping the point where the ball last crossed the hazard margin between himself and the hole. By so doing, he would be able to play over some trees blocking his line. May the player so drop?

_____(a) Yes.

_____(b) No.

3. In stroke play, a competitor is playing from just off the green. His fellow-competitor's caddie is attending the flagstick at the competitor's request. The player plays and the ball strikes the flagstick. What is the ruling?

_____(a) The stroke must be replayed without penalty.

_____(b) The ball shall be played as it lies; there is no penalty, because the stroke was played from off the green.

_____(c) The ball shall be played as it lies and the competitor incurs a two-stroke penalty.

_____(d) The fellow-competitor incurs a two-stroke penalty, as his caddie was attending the flagstick, and the competitor replays without penalty.

4. In match play, A's ball is 20 yards from the green. B's ball is 5 yards from the green in A's line. A, wishing to play a run-up shot, requests B to mark and lift his ball. B refuses on the grounds that A's ball would have to lie within two club-lengths of his (B's) ball in order for A to have the right to have his (B's) ball lifted. Is B right?

_____(a) Yes.

_____(b) No.

5. In any situation whereby a player may lift his ball under a Rule, the player may clean the ball before replacing, dropping or placing it.

_____(a) True.

_____(b) False.

6. A player drops a ball. The ball touches his shoulder en route to the ground. What is the proper procedure?

_____(a) The ball shall be re-dropped without penalty.

_____(b) The ball is in play and the player incurs a one-stroke penalty.

_____(c) The ball is in play and no penalty is incurred.

_____(d) The ball shall be re-dropped and the player incurs a one-stroke penalty.

7. In stroke play, a competitor's ball is on the green. He putts and his ball strikes the foot of his fellow-competitor's caddie, who was inattentive and was walking across the competitor's line unintentionally. What is the ruling?

_____(a) There is no penalty, and the ball is played as it lies.

_____(b) There is no penalty, and the ball is replaced and reputted.

_____(c) The fellow-competitor incurs a two-stroke penalty, and the ball is played as it lies.

_____(d) The fellow-competitor incurs a two-stroke penalty, and the ball is replaced and reputted.

8. A player is playing in the late afternoon. He has a 30-foot putt. He feels that some dew may have fallen, so he puts the palm of his hand down on the green several feet behind his ball to determine if the green is wet, and in the process, scrapes the putting surface. Is such procedure a violation of the Rules?

_____(a) Yes.

_____(b) No.

9. A player, after hitting his second shot, searches for his ball for a minute or two and does not find it. He returns to the spot from which he played his second shot and drops another ball under Rule 29-1. At that point his original ball is found and less than five minutes had passed since search for the original ball began. May the player abandon the dropped ball and continue play with the original ball?

_____(a) Yes.

_____(b) No.

10. A and B play their better ball against C and D in a match. The proper term for such a match is:

_____(a) Best ball.

_____(b) Better-ball of pair.

_____(c) Four-ball.

_____(d) Foursome.

11. A player in a match is dormie when he is four down with four holes to play.

_____(a) True.

_____(b) False.

12. In a four-ball match, A's ball is near the hole in a position to serve as a backstop for B, A's partner, who is preparing to putt. May C or D, the opponents, require A to lift his ball before B putts?

_____(a) Yes.

_____(b) No.

13. A player may not discontinue play for any reason without authorization of the Committee.

_____(a) True.

_____(b) False.

14. A player's ball lies in a sandy area through the green. There is a small mound of sand about six inches behind the ball. The player grounds the club only lightly; however, with his backswing he eliminates the small mound of sand. Is there a penalty?

_____(a) Yes.

_____(b) No.

15. A player's ball is on the bank in a water hazard well above the water line. However, it has just rained, and the ball is in a small depression on the bank and the depression contains some rainwater. The player claims that the rainwater is casual water and that he is entitled to drop out of the depression without penalty, dropping in the water hazard, of course. Is the player right?

_____(a) Yes.

_____(b) No.

16. A player, after a search of one minute, assumes his ball (Ball A) is in a water hazard, but there is no reasonable evidence to that effect. He drops another ball (Ball B) behind the hazard under Rule 33-2a and plays it. He then crosses the hazard and finds his original ball on the other side of the hazard in some rough. Less than five minutes has passed since he began search. What is the ruling?

_____(a) The player abandoned Ball A when he played Ball B. He continues with Ball B without penalty other than the penalty under the water hazard Rule.

_____(b) The player must resume play with Ball A. There is no penalty for having played Ball B, as it was an honest error.

_____(c) The player must resume play with Ball A. He incurs a two-stroke penalty for playing Ball B, as Ball B was a wrong ball.

_____(d) The player must resume play with Ball A. He incurs a two-stroke penalty for playing Ball B, as Ball B was played under a wrong Rule.

17. A player addresses the ball and starts his backswing. In the middle of the backswing the ball moves. He continues his swing and hits the ball. Is he penalized because the ball moved?

_____(a) Yes.

_____(b) No.

18. A player lifts his ball on the putting green and tells his opponent that he damaged the ball on the previous shot and is going to substitute another ball. His opponent looks at the ball and disputes the player's claim that it is unfit for play. The player claims he is the sole judge as to whether his ball is unfit for play. Is the player right?

_____(a) Yes.

_____(b) No.

19. A "rub of the green" occurs when a player gets a bad break such as when his ball comes to rest in a divot in the fairway.

_____(a) True.

_____(b) False.

20. A paved cart path is not an obstruction.

_____(a) True.

_____(b) False.

21. A ball is on the fringe of the green. It is overhanging the edge of the green but no part of it is touching the green. Is the ball deemed to be on the green?

_____(a) Yes.

_____(b) No.

22. A putter with a shaft adjustable for length is legal.

_____(a) True.

_____(b) False.

23. In a match, A by mistake starts with fifteen clubs in his bag. He wins the first three holes and, walking to the 4th tee, he discovers his error. What is the ruling?

_____(a) A is disqualified.

_____(b) A loses each hole on which he carried fifteen clubs; thus he is 3 down instead of 3 up at the 4th tee.

_____(c) A incurs a penalty of two holes with the penalty being applied to the state of the match at the time the violation was discovered. Thus, A is 1 up at the 4th tee.

24. A player by mistake plays his ball from a spot which is out of bounds. His opponent claims that A loses the hole for playing a wrong ball. Is the opponent right?

_____(a) Yes.

_____(b) No.

25. A player, playing to a blind green, asks a spectator who has just walked down from the green where the flagstick is located. The opponent claims the hole on the grounds that the player asked for advice other than from his caddie. Is the opponent's claim valid?

_____(a) Yes.

_____(b) No.

26. A player, playing in the rain, may not apply resin to the grips of his club to keep his hands from slipping.

_____(a) True.

_____(b) False.

27. A player brushes aside leaves on his line of putt with his cap. Is this legal?

_____(a) Yes.

_____(b) No.

28. Sand is a loose impediment on the putting green but not elsewhere on the course.

_____(a) True.

_____(b) False.

29. A's ball is in a lateral water hazard. He determines the point where the ball last crossed the hazard margin and drops his ball not nearer the hole three club-lengths from the point where it last crossed the margin. Before A plays, B, the opponent, tells A that he (A) should have dropped within two club-lengths. B claims the hole for violation of the lateral-water-hazard relief Rule. A acknowledges that he dropped in a wrong place, but he claims that he may correct his error by lifting his ball and dropping it in a right place without penalty. Who is right?

_____(a) A.

_____(b) B.

30. A white line defines an area of ground under repair. A ball lies on the white line, but no part of the ball lies over the inside edge of the line. Is the ball considered to be in the ground-under-repair area?

_____(a) Yes.

_____(b) No.

31. A and B are playing C and D in a match. Each side is playing one ball. The partners strike off alternately from the teeing grounds and thereafter they strike alternately during the play of each hole. Officially, such a match is called a:

_____(a) Foursome match.

_____(b) Four-ball match.

_____(c) Scotch foursome match.

_____(d) Gangsome.

32. There are only two regulations in the Rules of Golf governing golf balls—one restricts the size of the ball and the other the weight.

_____(a) True.

_____(b) False.

33. A player begins a round with thirteen clubs. As he did not exercise his right to carry fourteen clubs when he started, he is prohibited from adding another club during the round.

_____(a) True.

_____(b) False.

34. When a stroke-play event extends over consecutive days, it is not permissible to practice on the competition course between rounds.

_____(a) True.

_____(b) False.

35. In a match between A and B, A repairs a spike mark on his line of putt on Hole 4. B says nothing at the time but he begins looking through his Rules book, and after driving off the tee, B claims Hole 4 on the grounds that the Rules do not allow repair of spike marks on the line of putt. Is B's claim valid?

_____(a) Yes.

_____(b) No.

36. In stroke play, a competitor tees his ball slightly in front of the tee markers and plays. A fellow-competitor then calls the competitor's attention to the fact that he teed off from in front of the markers. What is the ruling?

_____(a) The competitor is penalized two strokes and returns to the tee and plays from within the teeing ground.

_____(b) The competitor must count the stroke played, return to the tee and play from within the teeing ground. The next stroke counts as his second.

(continued)

_____(c) There is no penalty, since the competitor teed off just slightly in front of the markers, and he continues play with the ball played from in front of the markers.

37. A ball lies just outside a bunker. A loose impediment in the bunker interferes with the player's stroke. The player is entitled to remove the loose impediment.

_____(a) True.

_____(b) False.

38. A ball lies in the rough. The player removes a twig which lies about six inches behind the ball. The ball does not move. A few seconds later, as the player is selecting a club, a gust of wind causes the ball to move. The player incurs a penalty.

_____(a) True.

_____(b) False.

39. In match play, a player and his opponent exchange balls during the play of a hole and it cannot be determined who played the wrong ball first. What is the ruling?

_____(a) The hole should be played out with the balls exchanged.

_____(b) Both players should be disqualified.

_____(c) The winner of the hole should be decided by lot.

_____(d) The hole should be considered halved.

40. A player's ball is picked up from the rough by a spectator who thought it was a stray ball. The spectator returns the ball to the player. Under the Rules, the player shall replace the ball on the spot from which it was lifted, but the spectator cannot recall the exact spot. The player drops the ball as near as possible to the spot from which it was lifted. Is the player correct?

_____(a) Yes.

_____(b) No.

41. In match play, a player's ball is behind a tree. He tries to play around the tree but the ball hits the tree, rebounds, hits the player and bounces into an unplayable lie. Is the player penalized because the ball struck him?

_____(a) No. In equity, there is no penalty, because the player did not benefit as a result of the ball having struck him.

(continued)

_____(b) Yes. The player loses the hole.

_____(c) No, because the player did not purposely allow the ball to strike him.

_____(d) Yes. The player is disqualified.

42. A player addresses his ball on the green. He steps back as a gust of wind comes up. The wind then blows hard and causes the ball to move. The player incurs no penalty, because he did not cause the ball to move.

_____(a) True.

_____(b) False.

43. A player cuts his ball with a skulled shot on the 4th hole but he does not notice that the ball has been damaged. He drives from the 5th tee and then discovers that the ball had been cut on the previous hole. May the player substitute another ball at that point?

_____(a) Yes.

_____(b) No.

44. A player's drive is hooked into high rough near a boundary. He hits a provisional ball in the fairway nearer the hole than the spot where his original ball presumably came to rest. He looks for the original ball for a minute but does not find it. He moves on to provisional ball and plays it. At that point, the player's caddie finds the original ball. What is the ruling?

_____(a) The player loses the hole, because he did not search for the original ball for five minutes.

_____(b) The player must abandon the provisional ball and continue play with the original, since he did not search for it for five minutes and therefore it was not lost.

_____(c) The original ball was deemed lost when he played the second shot with the provisional ball; he must continue play with the provisional ball.

45. During a match play competition, bad weather renders the course unplayable. In such a case the Committee has authority to suspend play and resume the matches from the points at which they were discontinued or cancel the round and start all discontinued matches over again.

_____(a) True.

_____(b) False.

46. A two-stroke penalty incurred by a player may not be waived in exceptional individual cases.

_____(a) True.

_____(b) False.

47. In stroke play, a competitor returns his scorecard to the Committee. The hole-by-hole scores are correct; however, the total for one 9 as entered on the card by the competitor is incorrect. What is the penalty, if any?

_____(a) No penalty. The Committee should correct the error.

_____(b) Disqualification.

_____(c) Two strokes. The Committee should correct the error.

48. In a four-ball match, a player putts and his ball strikes his partner's ball and moves it. What is the ruling?

_____(a) The player and his partner lose the hole.

_____(b) No penalty; the partner must replace his ball.

_____(c) No penalty; both balls are played as they lie.

_____(d) No penalty; the partner has the option of playing his ball as it lies or replacing it.

49. In a four-ball match, a player plays his second shot to the green, although an opponent's ball is farther from the hole. The opponent has the right to require the player to replay in proper order.

_____(a) True.

_____(b) False.

50. How many Rules are there in the Rules book?

_____(a) 37

_____(b) 52

_____(c) 41

_____(d) 39

_____(e) 46

ANSWERS

1-B (R. 31-2, 22-2c)
2-A (R. 33-3a)
3-C (R. 34-3a)
4-B (R. 24)
5-B (R. 23)
6-A (R. 22-2a)
7-B (R. 35-1h)
8-A (R. 35-1f)
9-B (R. 22-4)
10-C (Def. 28)
11-B (Def. 34)
12-A (R. 40-1b)

13-B (R. 37-6a)
14-B (R. 17-1)
15-B (Def. 8)
16-C (Defs. 5a and 5c)
17-A (R. 25-1)
18-B (R. 28)
19-B (Def. 27)
20-B (Def. 20)
21-B (Def. 25)
22-B (R. 2-2c)
23-C (R. 3)
24-A (Def. 5c)

25-B (R. 9-1a)
26-B (R. 37-9c)
27-B (R. 35-1b)
28-A (Def. 17)
29-A (R. 22-5)
30-A (Def. 13)
31-A (Def. 28)
32-B (R. 2-3a)
33-B (R. 3-1a)
34-A (R. 8-3)
35-B (R. 11-1a)
36-A (R. 13-2)
37-A (R. 18)

38-A (R. 27-1e)
39-A (R. 21-2a)
40-A (R. 22-3c)
41-B (R. 26-2a)
42-B (R. 27-1f)
43-B (R. 28)
44-C (Def. 6c)
45-B (R. 36-4c)
46-A (R. 36-5)
47-A (R. 38-2)
48-B (R. 40-1c)
49-B (R. 40-1d)
50-C

4

INDEX TO THE RULES

D

About the Authors

Tom Watson, winner of the 1977 Masters and the 1975 and 1977 British Open championships, was chosen Player of the Year for three straight years beginning in 1977. He is a graduate of Stanford University.

Frank Hannigan, Assistant Director of the USGA, has helped to conduct more than a hundred national championships and international competitions. He has a second career as a prize-winning golf writer and frequently appears as a special commentator on the rules of golf during network golf telecasts.